Contents

Dedication

This book is dedicated to four million small businesses, property owners and individuals who endlessly struggled with banks, finance lenders, courts, councils and lawyers. And to those who kept trying and yet came up short again and again against a greedy vicious system leading up to the pandemic. I salute all four million small business owners.

Sixty-six million people have a right to know what has really been going on behind the scenes in UK financial Institutions which have affected normal, average people.

It is also dedicated to 2.5 million military veterans and also to those 250,000 who continue to serve the nation either in the frontline or in their post military careers and their civilian business roles. You know who you are wherever you are.

Finally it is also dedicated to my own team who saved 56 injured soldiers by helicopter whilst we lost 34 men and women on our operation after 9/11. Those who died were the real heros. They were quiet, professional and exceptional, normal people who just gave every day, unlike the financiers who destroyed people and businesses when the pandemic struck. There really is another way and that way is better for everyone. These warriors and the country deserve better from the current financial system.

The financiers could learn alot from these incredible men and women who serve in the military and then go on to build their own businesses and pursue other ventures.

'Fat Sapper'

JPH

Acknowledgements

Thanks go to:

My family and my friends, and investors who have had to go through hell. You are real heroes. 'P', 'S' and 'S' you were quietly always there for me.

'JQ', 'MR' and 'SG,' I just wish I could have said goodbye. Gentlemen all.

Both my mother and father, who gave me and my sisters the best they could. My father taught me to fight. They had nothing and yet they gave me everything.

Late Squadron Leader Larry Parsons, Bradford Grammar School and Rank organisation. You gave me a chance.

Bedford College London University for shaping a rough farm boy for life. Always another beer in the Geography Department. I will get to a reunion one day.

8 Squadron Royal Engineers - 22 Engineers, Northern Ireland Regiment Army Air Corps, 847 NAS, 845 NAS and 846 NAS and Commando Aviation Helicopters whose leaders brought me back safely. My military diving and flight logbooks were always signed back in.

'Sappers' hurrah for the Chief Royal Engineer. Watch the film 'Zulu'. Lieutenant Chard VC.

Commando Training Centre. Respect for the Bottom Field - 'Green Berets'.

'Awkward' to any Military Diving Teams anywhere in the world. Dive safe.

Flying Colours who looked after me. Fly Safe. 'Down three greens for landing'.

Operation Raleigh for the adventure and exposure to the world. Explore safe. 'RR' RIP. Another Sapper John 'B-S' thank you for inspiring a generation.

Mentors and coaches in business and property who helped me. We all have struggled together since 2008/2009. Thank you for teaching an 'average' man.

Anyone who has tried and failed. Get back up and go again and again in the 'arena'. You have to for family, friends and for anything or for anyone worth dying for.

'The 34 and more, and the 56'. You were worth dying for. I tried my best.

'Fat Sapper'

JPH

Introduction

After 18 years in the military serving with the British Army, Royal Navy and Royal Marines Commandos in various specialist roles as a 'high average' soldier, I just wanted to be a force for good and try and help rebuild a small piece of Great Britain. My goal was to regenerate old, empty terrace houses, old MOD (Ministry of Defence) airfields, old hotels, breweries, warehouses and enable families and businesses to live in award winning homes and utilise commercial spaces. The locations I focused on ranged from Cornwall, Portsmouth, Bristol and Wigan in Greater Manchester. After the destruction and a form of reconstruction of sorts seen in Northern Ireland, invasion and subsequent six tours in Iraq, Beirut and Afghanistan it was time for me in my own small way to try and help rebuild the UK. I tried to help in terms of physical infrastructure, community, residential and commercial property as well as regenerating shops and pod offices.

This book is a true story of how an ex-soldier built 11 businesses worth £9 million over 12 years but then had it all completely destroyed by the banking and legal system. The system pulled all of the loans during COVID-19 losing £6 million of residential and commercial buildings and rents of £400,000 a year, ultimately losing all 11 small limited companies and sadly taking his family away from him and potentially losing his investors several million pounds in the process. He then took on the courts, the legal system, the financial and broker systems to whistle blow and expose what has been going on for years since 2009 to SMEs (small and medium-sized enterprises) and to property owners. He then methodically set about to get it all back for his family and investors simply as being the right thing to do. Assaults on site, threats to self, family, serious illness, blackmail, trolling and defamation and accusations of fraud made his resolve even stronger to take on the system and win. This is a simple David versus Goliath story. And a genuinely heart-rending personal account of how a basic raw human who was completely stripped down, came back from the very edge and blackest depths of despair. His determination to win against a greedy sinister and cancerous finance system, that had been building up since 2009 and then exposed by COVID-19 in March 2020, provided the fuel to write this book.

It is a frighteningly true story and many readers will be horrified at what fellow citizens will do to each other when financial stress is applied. It is especially appalling as this happened to someone with a military service background whose mantra since school was to serve the country and then go on to help small businesses and the property industry.

The reader will not put the book down until the very end realising that the human essence of fight or flight is in all of us to fight, win and survive against all the odds. Readers will be fully aware of the desperate situation of the 2008 financial crash that affected everyone in the UK. Recession, austerity, compliance regulation, Brexit and COVID-19 have all conspired to provide the perfect storm for small businesses to be destroyed by the banks, lawyers and courts, for no reason whatsoever other than pure greed and selfishness.

I will let the reader be the judge of the true horror story in the book and the incredible end result from a very personal 'why'. You will physically cry and laugh in equal measure in pure amazement at the actions of some highly intelligent yet incredibly basic, greedy human beings involved in finance. I have kept a diary for over 30 years and together with my military, civil flying and diving logbooks, travel and build site diaries, emails, hard copy letters and texts have forensically pieced the full facts together with the audited accounts. Of note, farm folk and military service persons tend to be quiet people in the background but I had to write this book to expose and get the truth out into the community to help to continue to serve my country and to right a major injustice to myself and my group of businesses. I am fighting for my financial life here and I know 100,000s of others are doing the same right now. This is *my* true version of events after the authorities tried to block its publication. I aim to help readers of the book who have suffered the same and can survive to fight another day in business. The business section starts properly in chapter 10.

To get the best out of this book look at the photo sections and captions first, it will really bring alive the personal story of Fat Sapper to be able to help you in your own lives and adversity to help you win. This will really help you to understand what has been going on in UK finance, especially since COVID-19. The story will amaze you and it is by any standards, unbelievable.

Enjoy the book. My mission is to help people. This is my story for my investors.

'Fat Sapper'

JPH

'It is not the critic who counts; not the man who points out how the strong man stumbles. or where the doer of deeds could have done them better. the credit belongs to the man who is actually in the arena, whose face is marred by dust and sweat and blood; who strives valiantly; who errs, who comes short again and again, because there is no effort without error and shortcoming; but who does actually strive to do the deeds; who knows great enthusiasms, the great devotions; who spends himself in a worthy cause; who at the best knows in the end the triumph of high achievement, and who at worst , if he fails, at least he fails while daring greatly, so that his place shall never be with those cold and timid souls who neither know victory nor defeat'.

Theodore Roosevelt

1

Seed of David vs Goliath – The Why?

This is a simple story of my starting from a Yorkshire Hill sheep farm in Bolton Abbey and ending up in the Crown Court after the banks pulled the lending on my businesses. This took away over 18 years military service, two years in Civil Aviation and 12 years of my graft and hard work in business, and a £9 million asset base in its entirety, and more. It included a £6 million property portfolio in the North West, a building and maintenance business, a coaching and mentoring business - 11 limited companies in total. These were all taken away from me due to the unnecessary greed and selfishness of the 'finance system'.

This story is about how the banks, courts and lawyers (as they have done in past recessions) just take good, basic small and medium-sized enterprises and destroy them immediately at the sign of any hardship. This is without any pragmatic forbearance or help to get through events like the COVID-19 pandemic. This was compounded by the fact that I had a lot of family's and friends' money as well as, civilian and military investors' money unsecured that the bridging companies, pensions, HMRC and courts were fully aware of and yet still crash sold losing over £1.1 million of property value and £1.5 million of limited company valuations. The fact was made even worse with increased lending fees of so-called unregulated bridging companies ranging from 16-27% APR during a time when the Bank of England base rate was 0.1% APR i.e. up to 270 times the lending rate. This resulted in a sad inevitable separation, losing the family home, all 11 companies and £6 million plus of property and being on a humiliating 'suicide watch' with the Wigan and Dorset Police forces and family doctor. All the driving force and reason for writing the book now is to show how the courts, lawyers, brokers, finance houses and banks have treated citizens before and during the COVID-19 pandemic.

Smashing into both private citizens and military veterans by the UK's so called financial and legal system was the line in the sand. Like General Ulysses Grant after the American Civil War who then became President of the United States, he lost all his money on an investment and wrote a book to get the money back which he did so. I am here also doing the same with 'Fat Sapper' being used with a media campaign. This book is a simple David and Goliath story. You decide the outcome of who was right or wrong and how we as individual citizens can rise up and fight and win against the system.

The story has been described as 'appalling' by people who have read and heard about it and every word is completely accurate and true. Every word is either on film, recorded or audited on email text and file. Real names have, where required, been changed for protection and legal purposes and any sensitive low level military material altered for specific operations and military personnel involved, to ensure the safety of everyone concerned. On the military side, any small low-level references to specific operations and to 'specialist troops' might include Special Forces and associated intelligence agencies. Throughout I will be just an average 'Fat Sapper' in the so-called Green Army world of Commando, Diving and Helicopter Aviation. My own military career by my reckoning was only 'high average'. I was only doing my job to the best of my ability, it was nothing special but I worked alongside people who were exceptional and world class and I thank them for bringing me home safely. I hope you enjoy the book which is 20% military and 80% business.

So what next? I had to get my integrity and confidence back and expose an industry starved of money putting so many SMEs under such unnecessary pressure. And I had to restore my name and reputation, get my companies back and get my family's, my friends' and investors' money back from the greedy lenders and associated lawyers and courts. Citizens for generations have always complained that this is just what the banks do. So why again now? The pandemic has changed the world from taking 10 years to produce a vaccine with 10 worldwide organisations who produced similar competing vaccines in just 10 months. Governments and health authorities changed overnight. People, the care homes industry, airlines, supermarkets, farmers, delivery drivers, office workers, stallholders and factory workers have all changed. Even terrorists around the world changed their method of operations.

Banks, finance companies and lawyers drew in the loans and smashed into individuals and SME owners yet again. Why did they not adapt and help like all other sectors? Instead we saw another generation of greedy financiers doing what they always have done. The BBC coroner's very sad report on the suicide case of Mike Norcross, the TV personality and property developer, showed the extremes and desperation of the finance lending in the UK which caused his death. I send my sincere condolences to his family. I know exactly what he was going through. Here 'Fat Sapper' challenges that status quo. The unusual farm and military background added at the start will give context of my military experiences which shaped me into who I became to enter into the business world and the fight to right a very big wrong later in my life which every UK citizen and even the very smallest business owners have a right to know.

2

The Farm, Boyle and Petyt, Bradford Grammar School and University

When I was two years old we moved from the rough areas of Colne and Nelson to a farm at Bolton Abbey in the Yorkshire Dales. Deep down, this was for me an amazingly varied life with a vast amount of physical work.

My father wanted the opportunity to take on a lease as a tenant farmer on 45 acres of a classical hill sheep farm which was about 900 foot above sea level. It was basically reclaimed moorland. As well as working the tenanted farm with my mother, he also worked out of Halton East Quarry as a tipper lorry driver. This was hugely busy and physical and at the same time very varied and seasonal which I personally really enjoyed. People living in towns seemed boring and restricted somehow to my simple mind. Dry stone walling, making hay and silage, raising cows, pigs and sheep, farm maintenance, and lorry driving and maintenance were typical duties, regardless of rain, sun or snow.

Dad was very physical and in many ways a very non-conformal, independent man while mum was the brains of the business and did all the paperwork. She previously used to do all the Hants and Dorset Bus company books before meeting Dad. I was a painfully shy child attending the local Boyle and Petyt country school whose benefactor was Robert Boyle of the Boyle's Law fame (ironically years later as an Army and Navy commercial diver we had to recite the pressure laws or face hundreds of press ups in the sea). I was the eldest with two sisters so when I was old enough I had to look after the girls as Mum and Dad were always busy. They loved it all despite the hard nature of life. Dad made sure I could drive tractors and HGV trucks as soon as I was old enough. He was the epitome of Yorkshire Grit.

The local primary Boyle and Petyt school was a very small parochial school. School kids from farms were pretty robust at best with most ending up as adults on farms, lorry driving or dry-stone walling or working for the Duke of Devonshire's Estate of which our farm was part of. We also had children from surrounding areas like Silsden and Draughton who I would have classed as village or town kids. Bolton Abbey had Bolton Hall with all the history of the Duke of Devonshire Estate which was great for school projects and I seemed to enjoy learning history and geography helped by a huge children's book about travel and other countries with lots of pictures of soldiers in fancy uniforms.

The farm business included newly bulling heifers which then produced a calf. We kept the calf if it was female and sold the heifers to lowland farmers who then milked the cows. Skipton Cattle Market was a big day out with a basic lunch if we did well or won a £10 first prize. From memory, red, blue and yellow tickets were awarded for first, second and third prizes. Mum and Dad gave five pence in the pound Yorkshire luck to the buyers of cattle and sheep if we got over a certain amount. When Dad passed away 30 years later 500 farmers came to the farm sale to give all his luck back. It is such a shame that later on in my life our society could not work this way. What goes around comes around. Like my father I would always be giving in the military but in business later this was not such an admirable trait.

I never saw my father write a letter but there was never a car, motorbike or aircraft that he did not know about and he had an amazing ability to 'plait sawdust'. He could do anything with nothing on the farm and could take an engine and gearbox apart without a manual. As I got older taking the lorry wheels off really kept you warm in the winter. He had six wheeler Foden lorries with Gardner engines so that meant 10 sets of tyres and a lot of hard work. I had a machine which cut out extra tyre treads to make them last longer. A Health And Safety Executive would have had a field day these days. We had friends with girls older than me so I had girls' shirts and jeans as hand me downs on the farm. Kids don't know any better. We could do so much with absolutely nothing.

Often we got hungry between meals so we would pinch cattle feed, oxo cubes and jelly cube sections on our walkabouts from Mum who would go nuts. Cattle feed pellets were like dry cardboard. I would regularly go onto the moor all day with my sisters and be told not to come back until tea. We learned amazing independence, resilience and initiative to go and do things down at the Bolton Abbey Strid (which is a particularly dangerous stretch of water). We would round up lost lambs and I would put them over my shoulder and bring them back.

The Eleven Plus came which I failed due to a glitch in the system and the headmaster, Mr Chadwick, made a big fuss and so I missed Ermysted's free grammar school at Skipton. Although I was always quiet I made a bigger commotion than my parents. Somehow I then ended up at Ghyll Royd prep with Mr Newman and boarded for two years to then get to Ermysted's Grammar which I did but I also passed the 13 Plus for the fee paying Bradford Grammar School.

I was not a major fan of boarding but once settled I really enjoyed sport and only got homesick on the release weekends at Prep. Dad would drive down on Saturday afternoons knackered and sleep in the car 'watching me'. I knew he was asleep but I never told him as I was just really happy with him just being 'there' as I knew how hard he worked for my school top up fees which I then paid back by the age of 18.

Mr Newman at Prep said Bradford Grammar was the better school with the prospect of University but Dad said no way due to the fees – we just could not afford it. Enter stage right, Mr DAG 'Dagsy' Smith, the Bradford Grammar School headmaster who revealed on interview a brand-new scheme which meant underprivileged kids could get a bursary from an unknown benefactor now known as the Rank organisation. The late Squadron Leader Larry Parsons was the Bradford Grammar School Rank liaison officer and was my first introduction to military servicemen. He was a lovely man and every recipient around the country spoke so highly of him as he affected so many peoples' lives by giving them a better chance in life. Larry and Rank I salute you.

I used to pray when I was at Bradford Grammar that Dad would be passing through with his lorry from work and pick me up and save me taking the bus. I told him about Latin verbs and studying Hitler and the periodic table which he nodded at, smiling and then telling me we had to muck out the cows and check the sheeps' hooves that night. It was a great balance and I craved, like my father, to be different and independent. Work hard, study hard, play hard.

Travelling two hours daily to get to and from Bradford Grammar and the sausage machine of 'O' and 'A' level cramming meant little time for sport. I used to envy the swimmers and rowers training – they seemed like monster men compared to my puny frame. Watching the future Olympian Adrian Moorhouse swim train for six hours a day filled me with both envy and admiration. I would get fitter and stronger lifting and stacking the hay bales during haymaking time and wrestling large lambs on the moor. I became a lifeguard at Skipton Baths where I would cycle a 14 mile round trip and get free swimming for two hours a day. I still sometimes swim two hours a day now for my own 'Olympic Gold' and to become stronger.

I started to get more confident and quietly much more competitive. Bradford Grammar seemed hard work but I gained the 'A' levels and ended up with a university place at Bedford College, London to read Geography specialising in units in Oceanography and Marine Morpho-dynamics under Dr Jack Hardisty. Jacques Cousteau was my hero and also a fictional Dirk Pitt penned by Clive Cussler. I still have the 'Dirk Pitt' orange faced divers watch today. Life certainly runs in full circles.

By the age of 18, I was a young man wanting to get off the farm and I was fully ready to leave and see the world. In the mid 80s, from memory, my grant was £1,950 per annum which meant I needed to work whilst at University, Bedford College, in Regent's Park, London. So I had to do holiday jobs at the farm as well as working at the local quarry mixing tarmac, working as a lifeguard at Skipton Baths and washing dishes at Betty's Tea Rooms in Ilkley. You may well remember the nation's hero, Captain Tom Moore? In his book you will find we both lived, worked, played and socialised in very similar areas separated by 60 years. I did anything to bring money in and I had to pay my parents half of everything I earned to pay off school support, board and food so it was really tight.

Three years at Bedford College in London merged with Royal Holloway in Surrey for my three year degree and I conveniently passed the selection for Operation Raleigh to go to Chile in South America. General Pinochet was the head in Chile at that time and an oppressive regime as we found out later. He was doing rather interesting things with his country in our presence. We were thankfully isolated on the icecap down south doing Oceanographic surveys ice climbing and then we rowed 300 miles to a settlement called Melinka which allegedly had emigres from Nazi Germany. On Operation Raleigh I again met more military people including Major Mark Bentinck from the Royal Marines Commandos Mountain Leaders. He made a big impression on me as did the Falklands War in 1982 watching the Army Paratroopers, the helicopter pilots, the specialist units and Royal Marines Commandos do the impossible. I was becoming more interested in military service and wanting to serve my country and to do Larry Parson, Bradford Grammar School and the Rank bursary scheme proud.

One last bit of adventure was after Operation Raleigh. I organised an expedition called Sahara 87 which was sponsored by Brigadier Ralph Bagnald, late of the Royal Engineers, founder of the Long Range Desert Group working with the SAS in World War II. Although he was a very old man then I had very interesting, private conversations with him which were fascinating. By the end of university I was fed up with having no money and I was ready to earn and go out into the world.

So what for business leaders? The 'service' ethic is important as I learned later. The military is all about the mission and teamwork but business is all about the bottom line. For both you need systems.

For my 'A 'levels you had to keep persisting. The challenge with the millennial mindset is they increasingly want instant gratification. But what cost does this have on persistence? As you will find out through this book I built up a £9 million property portfolio from scratch starting with £5. You can do so much with nothing and so few resources but you have to keep persisting and not take no for an answer. If you fail, start again, take another track and help other people. Always complete the mission, persist, be consistent and do what you say you will do. Good people will always be good and bad, selfish people will only be cancerous. Be in the company of great people, their greatness rubs off.

'The enemy knows this moment is coming too, some will have resolved to fight and others wish to survive. Be sure to distinguish between them. There are some who are alive at this moment, who will not be alive shortly. Those who do not wish to go on that journey, we will not send; as for the others, I expect you to rock their world. Wipe them out if that is what they choose. But if you are ferocious in battle, remember to be magnanimous in victory'.

Lieutenant Colonel Tim Collins

3

Military Service To Business

Bradford Grammar and Squadron Leader Larry Parsons, Operation Raleigh Leader Colonel John Blashford Snell, Chile Expedition Leader Mark Bentick, Royal Marine Mountain Leader and Long Range Desert Group Leader and sponsor Brigadier Ralph Bagnald meant it was the Army and the military for me. They all seemed like Gods to this rather simple farm boy. I walked into RMAS (The Royal Military Academy Sandhurst) and I was very nervous. My friends, Richard, Nick, Mike, Jim and Arthur, thought I was mad. It was an experimental graduate course condensed from 12 months into six months. It was also in 1987, so only five years after the Falklands War where so many Academy Staff were wearing Falklands and Northern Ireland Medals. They seemed like superhuman heroes to me. I felt very small next to them. As a non-guards sponsored Sapper who was not infantry, I was not really considered in the top flight group within the Sandhurst pecking order with its non-stop pace and little sleep for six months. I remember doing sport on Wednesday afternoons and falling asleep in the bath, waking up every Wednesday late evening in stone cold water every time. Knackered. After this, there was recognition that 12 months condensed into six months even by RMAS standards was asking a lot of both its cadets and training staff.

I excelled in only two notable times in my mind. The first five weeks you effectively do the route on the Pen y Fan in the Brecon Beacons and out of 40 groups mine was running fifth in the order. On the second to last checkpoint you did a final loop back up a mountain and then back down to the Directing Staff. They told my cadet group leader that due to the appalling and worsening weather they were going to halt the whole exercise for our group and for everyone behind, which our leader accepted. However, I jumped in and said I wanted to complete it which they then allowed us to do. I was really chuffed and it was a big tick in the box for me. The second leadership opportunity was Northern Ireland Training in the so-called 'Tin City'. This represented a base in Northern Ireland Bandit Country and the so called Irish 'Troubles' complete with watered down, real petrol bombs being thrown at us by trainees with opposing forces from within our Amiens Company. One of my exercise platoon leaders was an ex French Foreign Legion lad called Euan. He was a nice quiet boy who was leading us in the mock Northern Ireland Village when he was petrol bombed. However, the bottle had not been watered down and his combat trousers were ripped so his legs caught fire really very badly. The Directing Staff's fire extinguisher did not work so a group of us grabbed him and threw him in a roadside ditch which had mud and water in it. This did help him although he was still very badly injured. His Second in Command, an Education Corps chap, flapped a bit so I took over the platoon. I always tried to work outside the box.

RMAS Sandhurst was a quality place with quality people. The SNCO's (Senior Non-Commissioned Officer) at Sandhurst are just the best in the world. And in many ways they are the real backbone of the British Army with a genuine and very personal mission to ensure its officers command safely.

Also Colonel H Jones who was the Paratrooper CO killed in the Falklands - his son was commissioned in Amiens Company so the TV crews all flocked to him on parade. I was shoved to the back as my drill was poor hence the nickname, happy to 'Swerve to Lead' as we joked. I later went on to serve in the Falklands and to help build a swimming pool at Mount Pleasant. I stood at the actual spot on a Falklands Peat Bog where Colonel H died. Years later his son tapped me on the shoulder after we both completed the Belfast Marathon. He spoke in a thick Irish accent pretending to be the IRA - I nearly died. He was a very nice chap and very successful in a specialist Army role before leaving service. The last abiding memories of Sandhurst were oil paintings of two young men, Captain Nairac GC and Captain Westmacott MC. Each cadet that went through were in awe of these two young men serving in Northern Ireland who were both killed on live operations. Little did I know I would be piloting a Lynx Helicopter Gunship against the IRA in four years' time and then suffering a serious helicopter crash in South Armagh at a place called R23 in airframe ZD275. I once dived the Pacific Nuclear fleet at Bikini Atoll where you can see that the shipwrecks still have light bulbs unbroken from the 'Able' and 'Baker' nuclear test blasts. You can survive anything with mindset training and application.

So what? Don't be overawed by places, events and situations you think you are not capable of. Have confidence in yourself. As at the time of writing COVID-19 has knocked the stuffing out of the world and also out of many people who have understandably lost their confidence. And as we have hidden behind masks, mobile phones and computers we have missed the human trait of community and being in teams. We have all been struggling to get our mojo and our confidence back. My military training was a process of being pulled apart and then having a team build you back up. During COVID-19 so many, including myself, have tried to build back on our own which is harder as it is so easy to doubt whether you are doing the right thing. I found this very lonely. I treated COVID-19 as simply going to war which I did four times and was in one theatre six times. So I experienced numerous sets of exceptional circumstances which you had to continually adapt to.

After Sandhurst we had a period of leave then we went on to our Individual Special Arms training – Paratrooper to Pegasus Company, Commandos to the All Arms Commando Course, Gunners, Logistics, Drivers, Signals and 'Sappers' or Royal Engineers - the latter for me. The prospect of three years at London University, six months training at Sandhurst and then another seven months at RSME (Royal School of Military Engineering) in Chatham in Kent was not appealing to any of us graduates. On a short break after a few days it was obvious I was really ill with something following on from Sandhurst. I had contracted glandular fever. It took me the full seven months at RSME to recover, scraping through in watermanship, explosives and construction. Afterwards, I was posted to 8 Squadron 22 Engineer Regiment at Perham Down in Tidworth.

Major Keith 'M' was my squadron boss but we had a new Second in Command. He was a Paratrooper Diver Engineer who had just come off SAS selection on Officers week called Captain Stirling 'S' who took me under his wing. We had planned a troop commanders tour which consisted of six months in the Central America Jungle in Belize, Germany, a 'Cold War' exercise road deployment and a five month Falklands tour constructing a £1 million swimming pool. I had the opportunity to do both the arduous Royal Engineer Army Compressed Air Diver and Supervisor Commercial Diving Course. I modelled myself on Stirling who I named my boy after. Literally every day I was becoming more and more confident while getting much fitter. I used the Salisbury Plain area to get myself and my support troop very fit. It was a large troop with all the heavy construction plant and machinery for the whole Squadron. There followed six months in Belize with jungle training, interception of live drug trafficking, lurking patrols and diving on the reefs. A helicopter instructor's course in abseiling and access to all sorts of Army Navy and RAF (Royal Air Force) helicopters gave me a taste of maybe another future after an amazing period in Belize.

We deployed to Germany as a self-deployed Squadron road packet, with me in an armoured Ferret Scout Car with an upside down steering wheel. A Troop Commander got lost and hence the expression 'right grid wrong map sheet' was born. Germany and armour was a small experience for me remembering this was the Cold War against Russia.

The Falklands detachment for 8 Squadron was to be the culmination of my Royal Engineer Sapper time with a troop of 90 sappers building arguably the most exciting phase of a £1 million plus full 4 Squadron swimming pool project at Mount Pleasant Airfield. We had a civilian specialist contractor Ray and his workforce to do the mosaic pool tiling. He had an amazingly strong, small team who drank us under the table, won at arm wrestling and took all our money at cards in Port Stanley over four and a half months on the Islands. The swimming pool Army Royal Engineer team of Ray Butcher, Stuart Ness and John Furness kept me on the straight and narrow. On the island and indeed through time around the world Sappers on all detachments have a great reputation for hard work and making military life more pleasant for all three services. Construction and creating were some things I really wanted to do after the destruction of all sorts of war.

We started running night shifts to get back on schedule. Just like the farm I loved every minute of a large team effort and the General Officer Commanding, who was a Royal Marine, was really impressed with our work ethic. The whole Island seemed to be really impressed too. They were so interested in our hard work on 'their' Falklands pool as was Prince Philip on a visit. The construction phase on my Royal Engineer Young Officer course and my poor performance were now all fully vindicated by this fantastic, high profile, successful pool project and what I might go into after my military service. I even managed to get the Regimental dive team a diving task on the submarine HMS Osiris in the local Mare Harbour. In terms of variety, the Falklands and South Georgia out of 54 countries I have visited to date, have to be amongst the most interesting places I ever visited. The flora, fauna, history, whaling stories, the trade shipping wrecks including the SS (Steam Ship) Great Britain and all the wars have all affected the very friendly local people who survive the extremely harsh climate on a daily basis. This has shaped them into such a strong community just like Northern Ireland and Israel, politics aside.

My new boss Major Nick 'E' then allowed me to go to South Georgia on HMS Leeds Castle. Years later I asked Ranulph Fiennes to sign some books for my two children. I said my partner had been to the South Pole and I had been to South Georgia. His measured reply was 'South Georgia..... now that is a very interesting place'. Once I landed at RAF Brize Norton in Oxford I realised I had not seen a tree for five months - it was nice to be home.

So what? Teams and early career experiences set you up for life. You are who you socialise with, who and what you associate with and who you listen to.

In the military it was clear, even as a high average person, much of the selection of my immediate bosses and troops under command were superlative and this made a big impression on me. In war you see people at their best and at their lowest. It is the same in business. Some people have that natural knack of getting it all right, a good start in life, the right doors opening at the right time together with some luck and with natural networking abilities. Others just start wrong and never get out of trouble. They struggle, they have the wrong teams in place and associate with the 'wrong uns' and just keep coming off track too easily with bad luck. Mum and Dad were down to earth people but we were not street wise as farmers. Innocence and naivety can kill business.

How many youngsters do you hear of getting in the wrong gang? Later in my life after service I was struggling with a take-out branded business, in a northern coalfield town, called Fat Sapper - hence the name. This is where I saw first-hand the dreadful effect of drugs on late age teenagers with machetes and knives being cool. Here I saw the arrogance of entitlement where adults and police had no control and would use the excuse that 'they started out badly'. I, at the time, had two sets of clothes, a small rental flat, a 17 year old car with 150,000 miles on the clock, a phone and a laptop. After the banks pulled on me I was faced with losing everything, all properties and businesses and was living on £44 a day. I was recently separated and facing contempt of court and potential prison. These kids had £400 clothes outfits, they were getting taxis everywhere funded by drugs and I was on my hands and knees picking up their drug/cigarette butts, litter and cleaning their spit up at the Fat Sapper take-out. It was not so nice and it was one of many low points. I started with nothing yet had gained 11 businesses over 12 years and £6 million of property and lost it all thanks to the lenders pulling out money. These guys had everything but actually nothing at all if you get my drift.

Later during COVID-19 we had cars smashing into houses driven by drugged up drivers, machete attacks, motorbikes driving through shop windows, carjacking and ram raids in broad daylight. All these events were logged with Greater

Manchester Police but they never came to anything. I had just spent 12 years in the town building and regenerating and putting in more business rates and council tax on our occupied buildings. However, I was utterly dejected and disappointed. All these so-called leaders in the council, business groups, police, grants departments, and drug agencies had just given up. If we had had this type of leadership in the military, in Northern Ireland, Iraq, Beirut and Afghanistan we would have lost those wars. Everyone has seen the effects of poor leadership on the Afghan withdrawal. People can talk a great story - either do it and take action or be quiet. Be in the front line or not, either way, don't pretend, and be in the 'arena' fighting for your life. The real-world jungle is just that, adapt or die.

'The hand that gives is among the hand that takes. Money has no fatherland, financiers are without patriotism and without decency, their sole object is gain'.

Napoleon Bonaparte

4

Army Air Corps, Northern Ireland and Royal Marine and Royal Navy Squadron Life

In the British Army after your first tour as a Troop Commander you were offered a small innocuous black and white booklet called 'Further Opportunities for Army Officers'. It had a picture on the front of an SAS (Special Air Service) free-faller and inside pictures of helicopters and Army officers wearing unusual dress in far-away places. This was called a foreign loan service such as the explorer, then Captain Ranulph Fiennes, did in Oman. It was a bit like that children's book I had as a child with lots of countries and soldiers in uniforms in far-away places. The SAS after the Iranian Embassy siege in London in 1980 (one helicopter flown by a very good and inspirational friend Steve 'D' who would become a pilot mentor to me), Falklands footage and

Sandhurst exposure to Special Forces was interesting but instead I took the Commando Diver Helicopter route. I had completed 29 free fall parachute jumps in the UK, Germany and Belize and yet I thought I was not as natural as I was underwater.

The 'helicopter war' in Northern Ireland was about to heat up big time in the early 90s which I would become part of. Later, after 9/11 in about 2007, there would be over 400 helicopter crashes in Iraq and Afghanistan showing the inherent risk, and I had eight occasions where it was a really close call. It would become a very real and vital career especially as a rescue IRT (Immediate Response Team) 'Dust Off' rescue pilot. Saving lives using a helicopter in a combat zone has to be the best job in the world.

After getting back from South Georgia I managed to get some time off and give back to Operation Raleigh. This time I was a Jungle Instructor in Borneo which also included climbing Mount Kinabalu (13,435 ft.) on four occasions over three months. I caught dengue fever and lost three stone quickly but then three weeks later, after treatment by the Sabah Foundation, I was back climbing Kinabalu and back in the Jungle. Also around that time I climbed Mount Meru in Africa which is 14,980 ft and Mont Blanc in Europe at 15,771 ft. but started to get bad altitude sickness. I had climbed a hard route up Mont Blanc and I had no hot food due to kit failure - this was really unpleasant and not at all enjoyable. I am not a natural climber either and would catch viruses easily, glandular fever, dengue fever and later COVID-19.

After the Sappers a good friend, Captain Nick 'R', went flying training with the AAC (Army Air Corps) at Middle

Wallop so I thought I would give it a go. The next year and a half was really intense with the threat of being 'chopped' literally every day or night. Being chopped is a military term for the risk of coming off course. I was transitioning from fixed wing Chipmunks to Gazelle helicopters and then Lynx utility gunships or TOW (Tube-launched, Optically tracked, Wire-guided) missile aircraft. The AAC were a very nice family and very sociable, just like the larger Sappers Corps. This military family thing was maybe naively a big thing for me in my life like the Royal Marine Commandos and Royal Navy families later on.

Dusty 'M', Ian 'B', Paz 'N' and Bruce 'S' were my instructors, all flying gods in my mind as they dragged me backwards through flight training and got me my AAC wings. During my time they had a colour system of grading flights - a sort of 'dodgy tartan' blue, green, brown, red in order of success. Red meant you had to do the trip again or then fail. I broke my wrist so ended up rejoining the next course. I was not the best pilot by far but maybe was the most reasonably consistent which led me to the Lynx gunships in Northern Ireland.

The Northern Ireland posting for two and a half years for the quiet Yorkshire farm boy was where I began to grow up quickly. At the time of writing 1,440 soldiers were killed during the 'Troubles' involving 250,000 troops on Operation Banner which also affected so much of Mainland UK. The 'helicopter war' became pretty serious very quickly and over the next year Captain Carl 'P' Lynx was shot down and previously Captain, Sergeant George 'H' Gazelle was also shot down and a Puma collided in mid-air with a Gazelle at

Bessbrook Mill killing the RAF crew. Bizarrely the Gazelle guys lived having been thrown clear, one was an ex-Sapper chap. A large Chinook helicopter with all special force troops on board crashed into the Mull of Kintyre in thick fog killing all 29 passengers. It was big news at the time so it set back the Northern Ireland intelligence capability years due to the VIP's on board.

Another Lynx caught fire and crash landed soon after. They were all lucky to get out alive - the crash was caught on camera. A Puma got shot down out of New Town Hamilton with Flight Lieutenant 'D' rightly getting an award for saving everyone. I lost a tail rotor crashing a Lynx ZD275 at night at an Observation Post called R23 outside Forkhill in South Armagh. The handling pilot Captain Steve 'G', a qualified Helicopter Instructor who was instructing me into the Province, saved my life through his quick immediate actions. There is risk in everything so you have to train and keep your wits about you. It is the same in business.

I was also given the Door Gunner Flight to command with 15 door gunners operating the GPMG 7.62 machine gun with WO2 Gordon 'B' and Corporal Paddy 'R' making it another best job in the world with some superb guys. Firing sniper rifles from a Lynx in a 40 knot wind at 500 feet with a specialist team was an unusual profile job for me and my own Door Gunner crews who were involved. We also had Heckler Koch 53's - a much better personal weapon than the standard Army issue SA 80 weapon. Pilots like Major Bloo 'A' and Staff Sergeant Chas 'C' could do things with a Lynx that no one else could do. This included going upside down (very unintuitive), hovering in poor weather and flying up mountains to pick up troops.

Considering I did not want to go out to Northern Ireland and effectively crash due to a tail rotor failure within the first two weeks after two and a half years, I can safely say it was the best flying job in the world. I had the best friendships in the world and received the best of all the UK military forces had to offer. Captain Michael 'N', an old 8 Squadron friend, kept my feet on the ground even if he drove worse cars than me. This was a continual joke back at 22 Engineer Regiment days at Perham Down. It was genuinely an amazing time and apart from '400' hard core terrorists the local Irish folk were equally fantastic and so friendly and we were all, after the Good Friday agreement, so very very pleased that peace came at last. Northern Ireland was an amazing time in history and an amazing place to be part of with the best of the UK Forces servicemen and women who still continue, to this day, to be the best in the world.

One rather sad occasion, a story with a great twist, was a civilian car crash. A car got T-boned at a busy crossing by a large HGV articulated lorry deep in Bandit Country in South Armagh - at that time it was one of the most dangerous places in the world. The parents sadly died immediately with the two small children seriously injured in the back. Then sadly soon after, the other child died, so it was our task to save the other small girl. We were on routine helicopter patrol oddly as a single ship aircraft; usually we had to fly in formations of three aircraft because it was so dangerous down there.

The problem was that the civilian hospital in Newry was seven miles away but the roads in all four directions were now totally blocked with backing up traffic. We had an Intelligence team on board so my pilot aircraft captain Warrant Officer 2 Bill 'W' immediately landed right on the crossing where the lorry had smashed into the car. Without a thought he said to the young Corporal Door Gunner, who had a Browning Side Arm Pistol with only 13 rounds (bullets), go and take the first aid pack (which clearly had the Red Cross showing on it) and render assistance.

That Door Gunner to this day was the bravest boy I have ever seen and had big balls of steel and never ever questioned his orders. The people in the cars and the general crowd were clearly very angry and upset at the situation. It looked like we were the enemy and clearly not wanted at all. Once we found out the other child had died and the first aid kit was produced, the offer to take the other seriously injured child, who was still being cut from the car, to Newry by helicopter made it clear we were the only option to save her life. The crowd's anger, the atmosphere and threat dissolved immediately and everyone including the British Army, the IRA 'players', the local farmers, the police and the fire and ambulance crews worked together to save the young girl's life. We took off and saved her life with Newry being only five flight minutes away damaging some cars in the car park. That evening the British Army sent a teddy bear to Newry hospital and the IRA I believe sent flowers to RAF Aldergrove to my helicopter crew. The next day the bombing and shooting carried on - it could only happen in Northern Ireland! Folk are folk. You can do so much with so little but so much more when with good people.

The two and a half years seemed to pass quickly and as

usual I was always too focused to worry about settling down. With my Royal Engineer cap badge on a light blue AAC beret, I still kept in date as an Army diver with the Royal Engineers doing commercial military diving searches looking for weapons and bodies out of 25 Engineer Regiment at 'M' barracks. Sometimes I carried out helicopter diver drops too.

Major Dick 'H' came out to Northern Ireland as the boss of 3 Brigade Air Squadron and I chatted to him about doing a flight commander attachment with the Royal Marines and Royal Navy. I really wanted to do the coveted green beret Commando Course. Major Dick 'H' was one of the pilots during the Falklands War who flew a Commando Sea King all the way to mainland South America from the Falklands to land Special Forces troops. This was a massive aviation feat in itself. He was a real legend and his Aircraft Captain too. I personally was always high average yet these other military folks mentioned and those I served under were really the very best in the world. Our country needs more of these boys and girls to go on to lead and do good for our nation in other careers.

I was once very lucky to be taken to a place in London where there are records of people who served very quietly and in very specialist units since WWII. Some survived and some did not and it is amazing how many young SOE (Special Operations Executive) girls involved gave their lives. It was a very sobering place. I often look at how people in society who just take and take welfare whilst others just give to their country and just keep giving even to the ultimate sacrifice which is often very quickly forgotten. It is a game of two halves - givers and takers. This is a continuing theme of the book.

Years later I talked to a Spitfire pilot who privately showed me his pilot logbooks where he was also a Lysander pilot putting some of those young SOE girls into France with the French Resistance and some of whom did not come back. That hour I had with him rates as one of the most interesting of my life. He was a *real hero* and so modest as all these people always are. I was not talking to an 85 year old war hero, I was talking to a young man back in his 20s reminiscing about how scared he was, as all military personnel are at times in combat - I know I was. He was a very nice man to me. He really touched me and it was him and others that inspired this book, along with my frustrations of the leadership shown in finance and legal circles during COVID-19, where people just took and never gave.

Two examples in leadership are 1939-1945 with the Nazi threat of invasion building against Great Britain, and in 2021 the Taliban rising against the Afghanistan government following a poorly thought out drawdown. In 1939-1945 the leadership in all walks of life stepped up to the plate and despite huge odds beat Nazi Germany with great teams, alliances and relationships. In Afghanistan the leadership displayed by all walks of life completely failed their people in 2021, there was no teamwork and exceptionally good people were put at risk. In severe and critical situations like war, pandemics, recessions and depressions genuine leaders are shown up, good and bad. It is all about mindset.

Financial leadership during the pandemic was very poor hence my writing this book to expose this as well as the lawyers, courts, Government regulatory investigation teams and in some cases the police. In 2020 -2021, teamwork and any ability to repair and overcome the odds were completely ignored by the banks, finance houses and legal teams yet their profits soared. They chose to 'flee' as well. I might not be General Ulysses Grant from the American Civil War but my mission is exactly the same from this book as was his own book to get investors' money back. General Grant paired up with Mark Twain who cleverly marketed his autobiography and saved Grant's family from destitution. This was an inspiring action indeed. What goes around comes around in war and peace.

Likewise Bob Mason's book, 'Chickenhawk', was written for the exact same reasons about his experience in Vietnam as a helicopter pilot. This is an engaging must read for any aspiring military helicopter pilot with its descriptions of *human nature* when tested to the limit. It is a fantastic read.

I hope this inspires and helps those who got destroyed financially. For this Army and Navy Commando the next fight for my life is now on as you will see in the main part of the book. In war and terrorist operations the enemy can be very clear and very one dimensional. I did not expect to come back from serving the country to be then attacked by my own so-called countrymen in finance, courts and legal circles. The pandemic for me brought forward some incredibly greedy and selfish people and it did not need to be this way.

5

Royal Marines Squadron and Commando Training

I welcomed the move from Northern Ireland to RNAS (Royal Naval Air Station) Yeovilton to escape the pressure and being on duty for over two and a half years in Province. I enjoyed it hugely and was there for two years. As it turned out 3 BAS had changed its name and reformed into 847 NAS (Naval Air Squadron) which was an admin exercise effectively. I think the Royal Marines were not too impressed though. The eight week All Arms Commando course was to fall in the middle of the two year tour. The time on HMS Ocean, the helicopter carrier, was hugely varied as it also was on HMS Ark Royal and HMS Illustrious as well as RFA (Royal Fleet Auxiliary) shipping including RFA Olna and RFA Argus. I think the divers and aircrews managed to dive and fly off all the fleet shipping in accordance with the SHOL's (the helicopter regulations stating wind and sea state conditions to land and take off). We worked hard to work the deck up day and night with Lieutenant Dave 'W' helping me on ex-Purple Star to the USA then onto the Caribbean after on an Atlantic 'float' training up to invade North Carolina with the United States Marine Corps including a huge 200 helicopter night assault led by our aircraft.

Later on 'floats' (a float is a voyage e.g. Atlantic float) in the Mid Atlantic I remember one night with Lieutenant Adam 'S' one of my new pilots picking all the ships' captains up. This was called a SOOTAX (Senior Officer Transfer) for a meeting with 'Flags'. (Flags is the senior flags officer at sea).

It was a foul night and we had to land on a very tight deck with night vision goggles. The pilot's eyes had to, and at all times, stay glued to the instruments checking the engines, the gearbox and the fuel. You had to keep nodding left and right and to keep your references in the heavy swelling sea, and you also had to judge the deck and land on the 'bum line' at a right angle to the flying pilot's right hand seat. We had to land like this as the approach was made from the port (left) side of the ship. Imagine this and include the added pressure of having all the fleet management on board!

You also had to keep an eye on diversions as we did not want to ditch at night with high value VIPs on board. (If something does go wrong and a helicopter cannot land and has to ditch or divert to land or the nearest shipping dock, this is called 'black deck'.)

This was one of the most challenging flights I ever had and Adam went green and threw up in the end. Poor lad - it was a very hard night's flying.

On another night, an appendicitis nearly had us flying Mid Atlantic to Halifax Nova Scotia using another single ship 'lilly-padding' as a refuel point 180 minutes flight time in appalling weather. Thankfully the casualty settled and we were stood down. Helicopters are just an amazing and vital invention.

Also a big highlight was a winter Arctic Norway deployment at Fagernes on Gazelles including survival training wearing Arctic kit down to minus 20°C with us jumping into a frozen lake then rolling in the snow near naked afterwards to warm up! Then we camped out before being allowed to fly into the mountains. The attachment was for Gazelle helicopters but a Lynx pilot became ill after Norway and as I was already Lynx qualified I was given 'B' Flight, a Lynx flight to command. This flight I commanded under two Royal Marine Commanders Major Andy 'W' and Major Mike 'E', both were great guys and whose Squadron made me really welcome. My Army diver qualifications were transferred as well as my 'Ships Diver' and 'Supervisor' qualifications. This meant we could check in in any harbour in the world and do all HMS and RFA ships' maintenance and limpet mine checks and also keep our hours up. The diving pay hours were paid like the flying pay.

Once back in the UK in my own time I got out onto Woodbury Common and Dartmoor in the south west near Exmouth, Devon before the Commando course. I did this day and night to get fit with a loaded bergan (a rucksack) and recce the areas ready for the course in September to November. It was clear that at 32 (there were three of us that age) including a USMC (United States Marine Corps), Major 'Kz' and Paratrooper Gunner Sergeant Major 'Bart' 'S'). I was not a youngster. There were many 18-22 year olds from the Sappers, Gunners, Aircrew, Logistics and drivers aka 'Tarts and Vicars' All Arms Course Commando Course. Unlike many others who had done a 'beat up' i.e. three weeks of pre-course training, I was a little unfit after being stuck on ship. So I had to get going quickly at the CTC (Commando Training Centre).

The first half of the course is on Woodbury Common on an old chemical range which still has chemicals in the ground. This I did not enjoy too much as you could get infected from scratches from the gorse. Then onto Dartmoor which I much preferred with the wide-open spaces interspersed with Top and Bottom Field Criterion tests at the CTC which have remained unaltered since 1941. You pass or fail, black or white. Although the weather could be really foul I never got cold in two months as you were always running everywhere.

At the All Arms Course we had our own area in the barracks and we were kept apart from the Royal Marine main area; Captain JT 'V' with Sergeant Dave 'L' were the directing staff. The course is described as 'extremely arduous' compared to other world specialist courses and I eventually became fitter. One thing I did note that in the field we did PT actually on exercise which was fine. You would be called to stop, make safe, then clear your machine gun weapon (the SA80) and then go on to do PT. They had a process on field inspections of checking weapons and bergans first thing and if they were not up to standard you would be quietly taken to the side, to the 'flank Sir', and then beasted for more exercise whilst the others could get breakfast and relax. I liked the fact that it was not a 'shouty' place. I liked the Marine quiet approach rather than basic training recruits, when they needed to they really shouted. I was pretty meticulous after Sandhurst and my other courses but got flanked every single time which frustrated me. We had an SBS (Special Boat Squadron) Corporal 'E' who was a real tough lad and with a quick 'wink' I realised my kit and standards were spot on. They were just getting me fitter each morning every day to pass by the extra 'flanking' exercise. It worked and I eventually passed. It was a really varied course and the officers were given extra orders and work to run the exercises which I found OK. The real test was the mindset of not failing when exhausted and getting no sleep. It was two months of solid running around and ensuring you did not fail each measured Criterion Commando test. It was nice to jump into a helicopter from our units and get warm for 10 minutes and get a big smile from the Navy Junglie and Marine pilots watching over us.

The rope work seemed to phase a lot from the Army and the 'sheep dip', the tunnels, the Tarzan assault and the bottom field obstacles were all quite a test of the mind to make sure you made it every time. We lost about a third of the team. Interestingly these were a lot of the lads who had done the 'beat up' but who were just absolutely worn out too early. On rest Sundays I would peel my blisters off and pour on raw iodine. I screamed at the pain but this treatment worked well.

I liked learning about the foreign weapons from G3's, Ak47's, Uzi sub machine guns to Walther pistols, the latter with their drilled out magazines to lighten them which was all hugely interesting and then to fire them all on the range. Eventually we got through the eight weeks and the last day culminated in the dreaded 30 mile speed march (a herd of elephants would not have stopped anyone passing now) with light webbing and weapons complete with a rather funny tradition of a Cornish pasty stop half way along. What was really nice was the last few miles when a representative from your own sub-units Commanding Officer or Second in Command would join in and run to the finish where you were presented with your green beret. I remember Lieutenant Commander Paul 'M' bringing a bottle of champagne down. It involved good friends and teamwork again.

Walking into 847 NAS The Commando Helicopter Squadron rates as one of my proudest days up there with Sandhurst, the Army Divers course along with my AAC Wings (outside of my marriage and two children later in life). The squadron was very friendly when I first arrived. There was a really quiet and deep respect and I think that I was now fully accepted - everyone shook my hand off. It meant so much and for once I felt a fully grown-up man and I knew Stirling 'S' would have been really proud.

We were UK bound then for a few months then off to the Far East on ex-Ocean Wave on a Royal Fleet Auxiliary, not a Royal Navy ship, effectively for a very large exercise. This included jungle work in Brunei visiting Gibraltar, Djibouti, in Singapore dodging the pirates at sea out on the straits, and also supporting the Hong Kong close down. The Hong Kong close down looked to me like the empire was slowly closing. My ship broke down with a broken drive shaft in Singapore at Sembawang and I stayed on board and studied for my airline exams next door to HMS Britannia. Rather nicely some evenings, I was hosted by their ships' officers. Resupply at sea RAS was where two ships would sail together 100 feet apart as the fuel was pumped across, and why Britannia got damaged in the first place.

It was interesting to hear how her ship's company said how hard Princess Anne and other Royals worked on their Royal Duty deployments - this stuck in my mind. I was lucky enough to meet The Queen, Prince Philip, The Queen Mother, Princess Diana and Prince William over the years as most soldiers tend to do in odd situations. I apologised to the Queen at the time for crashing one of her helicopters which seemed to annoy her Equerry but she smiled knowingly. You sign a helicopter form from a F700 book when you go flying which shows that technically the helicopters belong to her! Only in the services, the Royals - such great ambassadors for the country. William and Harry are also superb ambassadors for the younger military.

My time in the military was then due to come sadly to an end after an extension of my short commission to 10 years. Over the holiday period, like my other pilot friends, I was working on my Airline and Helicopter Commercial Licences which meant two sets of exams of nine navigation and five technicals plus about 150 odd hours building over in Florida in a Cessna 150 puddle jumper. I still remember the registration, c/s N4702X, which is your Air Traffic Control call sign. Then I moved onto a twin-engine Beech 76 for Instrument flying, the so-called 'Twin IR'. This is the hardest flying I have ever done with ex-Navy man, Brian Marinden, at Exeter airport - a lovely bloke and 'magician' who managed to get me a pass. God knows how. It all cost me £14,000 which today would cost you over £140,000 to train a scratch pilot. Brian had an amazing knack of not getting a military pilot to fly one minute more than they needed too. He really helped to keep the costs down as otherwise they would have been astronomical. He was another amazing man.

A great friend SFO (Senior First Officer) Gary 'B' was working for a new venture capital airline called Flying Colours which was headed up by Errol Cossey. It employed ex-managers and ex-pilots from Air 2000 (a British charter airline that operated for 17 years between 1987 and 2004). Gary and I knew deep down that I really wanted to stay in service and fly the bigger Sea King Commando Junglie aircraft and transfer my commission from Army to Navy but the civilian airline job was there on offer.

I was all dressed up in a blazer and tie with all my licences plus I had my military logbooks for flying, military and diving, plus my green beret and medals and I went to see the Royal Navy 'Appointer'. He was also nicknamed the 'Disappointer' for obvious reasons. Civilians would name this nowadays as 'Human Resources'. This was my last desperate visit. I tried everything to try and stay in service but his answer was still no. I was in equal measure angry, totally disappointed and deflated. This would also later happen in my business world. As I left with my tail well and truly under my legs I turned to him and asked when he was due to be posted. 'In two years, young man,' he said, to which I replied, 'I will do two years with the airline, Sir, and then I will ask your successor to give me my commission back when you have left'. I saluted and walked off. People in authority who command and who are in positions where they have the ability to influence peoples' lives, just like the banks, should try to help every time. I have absolutely no time for those who do not.

So what? Variety is the spice of life but it is important to keep a sense of balance of work, family and life. In the Army and Marines there are expressions called 'Army Barmy' and 'Corps Pissed' which means people get so involved and focused and go after the career too much - as they do in business. I did just this to the detriment of my personal life. On operations and in war it becomes very one dimensional and focused for the person in the arena which is easy. Partners I think suffer a lot in service. A good friend, Captain Zac 'N', wisely said 'It is great to be an action man warrior in the military, but remember you are just a finger in a bucket of water; when pulled out see what is left' i.e. you can only do such much in life so it is fundamental to have balance. He was a wise man.

'The world breaks everyone and afterward many are strong at the broken places'

Ernest Hemingway

6

Airlines

The next day I accepted a Senior First Officer slot at Flying Colours flying Boeing 757's out of Manchester. I had the car filled to the brim at the age of 33 with everything I had and a trailer with an antique BMW motorbike. I then got a ticket from the police. I said to myself 'yesterday I was a warrior, today I am a criminal'. That exact wording would be uttered nearly 18 years later over a business fiasco due to the banks destroying me and my family. This is the reason for writing about the farm and military service first for you to get a measure of my persona before we get into the main story about the business career and the Brexit and COVID-19 damages.

Once settled, near Bentham in the North West, in a small new build house, I signed with Flying Colours with Adrian Richards, Tim Bull and Greg Turner for my Boeing 757 fleet. They were all great guys. The airline had seven 757's and with each new airframe the airlines were given free simulator training slots which pilots paid for, worth £24,000 from memory, and were bonded for two years (perfect for my plan). The airline years later would end up as Thomas Cook with 34 aircraft before Royal Bank Scotland refused them a loan and they went into administration - more on this later. I went to Seattle to the Boeing 'Yellow Barn' where the company started. It is now no longer there and I had four weeks in the simulators. I worked very hard with little time off but managed to see and go up the Seattle Needle. This is an iconic 605 ft. tall spire at the Seattle Centre with an observation deck and a rotating restaurant. Our female instructor, Karen, gave us a Boeing 757 silver pin badge. It was all very professional and corporate.

After that we went back to the UK and we each had 60 minutes with our own 757 flying landings and take offs at Liverpool airport. The next trip and subsequent line training was then with 235 passengers en route. I must admit the first six flights you wondered how the hell the aircraft had taken off and landed. There was so much going on - flying at Mach 0.82 or 82% of the speed of sound which varied at set altitudes. It was busy, then it clicked, and the automation all started to set in. The airline was a typical short to medium haul outfit carrying nothing glamorous with 'Club 18-30' and Thomas Cook typical chartered clients. For the first year typical routes would be to fly out, land, spend 45 minutes refuelling and then return. There was no travel abroad outside of the airport. This was not quite the variety that we encountered in the military as this involved flying to places such as the Canaries, Greece and Turkey, Ibiza and winter ski resorts. I was very disciplined and made sure my military reserve commitment was kept up to date, flying Gazelle helicopters, keeping the Green Beret military criterion Basic Fitness Test and Complete Fitness Test fitness levels up and the military diving and supervising in date. I had to be very, very careful with getting the bends flying after diving. It was OK until flight operations started to mess the roster around.

I quickly realised that with the automation of civil flying and shift work, I was craving travel, excitement and variety. I had had this at the farm, in the military and my previous teams with everything revolving around work. Here I was being a shift worker with not really many other duties or responsibilities. After a military commission I found life very boring, not helped by not being settled down or married.

Zac 'N' was proving to be right. Also in two years we had massive disruption merging with several airlines - Peach Air, Airworld, Caledonian then becoming JMC (John Mason Cook was Thomas Cook's son). It later became just Thomas Cook.

It got to a stage in my second year where airline pilots not under training caught the night slots so I would regularly do two night Canaries flights in a row from the UK out and then back overnight both Thursday and Friday night. Then I would always be rostered for standby on Saturday night - and I was *always* called out for a night Canaries flight i.e. three nights in a row of flying. This involved 12,000 miles flying over three nights week after week. It was totally exhausting and not glamorous in the slightest. It was the equivalent of flying half way around the world in three nights. Union rules stated that you were not allowed to have three night flights rostered but being given a standby duty and then to be called out was acceptable. For some reason I found this really annoying and unprofessional on the management of the pilots. Why not treat people like adults? It was the system and the contracts and unions being made paramount as opposed to individual actions. I still hear pilots today talk about roster stability and the inability to plan and night flying being the main gripes - certainly in charter flying.

Crews were getting exhausted and you could never plan anything. My running, say on a 45 minute set route circuit, I would add an extra 20 minutes due to fatigue and exhaustion. However, I still kept professional and got on with it and was lucky at the end to get a Command Recommendation after 22 months which is normally issued on performance in the simulator.

I had a few interesting airline moments, fun, odd and historical. Three specific instances stand out. As I said I was a high average pilot both military and civil and although I found airline flying too automated for me, we did have the odd minor emergency like iced up flaps and electrical and weather gremlins. I did however enjoy the dispatch and landings and simulators due to the pressure and workload. Also we did several CAT 3B landings which means the aircraft can match its automated equipment to certain airfields and land in full fog and come to a full stop itself. This was really amazing. You just had to really keep an eye on the 'raw' data and make sure the plane was where it was supposed to be on the beacons. These airline fog landings and take offs would be of use later in my life. Someone once told me you earn your flying pay once a year.

I flew to Bahrain and India twice and once on the return I elected to divert into LGW (London Gatwick) and refuel then head back up to Manchester in poor weather. It was a long day and we were working hard. We were on fumes at LGW and at 42,000 feet I could 'glide' at three times the altitude i.e. 126 miles. The normal convention was that the other pilot goes out to do the fuel which you manually do with a ground handler under the right wing. However, this time with Club 18-30 onboard the Captain asked me to do it. Once I opened the door to go and refuel I realised why he said this as 235 passengers booed and threw paper cups at me. He was an experienced Captain! The same happened to me after I got back on after refuelling. It was a long night that one back to Manchester. I smiled - what a glamorous industry.

Once we had a normal standard flight to Tenerife South and as we landed it was my turn to refuel. Oddly we parked next door to Concorde - it was not a usual location for that aircraft. I gladly refuelled which took a long time (as it was over 1,800 miles back so we needed many tonnes of fuel). As I waited outside I noticed a lot of rubbish on the tarmac which included metal items such as broken prams and things which I picked up and more importantly 'oggled' at and walked around Concorde. It is such an amazing aircraft. With the refuelling over I went back and the captain gave me a bit of a hard time over my delays and asked why I had the metal in my hand. I explained on aircraft carriers we always pick up FOD (Foreign Object Damage). He said airports are always like this. We took off and thought nothing more of it. Years later on 25th July 2000 Concorde crashed in France after some metal work/FOD damaged her underbelly tanks killing everyone on board and sadly also the Concorde dream. Years later I started dating a girl and it turned out that her father was the Concorde pilot back in Tenerife whose aircraft had broken down. Life goes in circles, make sure you know where yours are. Attention to detail and lack of it can kill whether in the military, aviation or business.

On another occasion the purser asked the captain if we could host a nervous flyer. The man in question was a big tall man but I have never seen anyone more frightened in my life. He stood and held on with white knuckles. I started to chat to him to calm him down saying I used to be scared of flying and showed him around the cockpit explaining what each dial did, etc. I asked him what he did, the usual chatter, and it turned out that he used to be a Royal Engineer (a Sapper). He told me he had completed eight and a half years, which I thought was an unusual engagement time, so I asked why he left. He then dropped a bombshell saying he was in the Kegworth air crash disaster in 1989 when the crew had shut down the wrong engine. You can still see the mark on the M1 motorway where 47 out of 118 died. The Captain then perked up a bit. What then happened was quite extraordinary as it was clear he had never properly talked to anyone about it and he just blurted it all out - it was totally amazing. Ten minutes later he was 'right as rain' and had a cup of coffee with us. That one was the best civilian flight ever by far. Sometimes people need to talk and you need to listen.

I took my father flying to Tenerife and he was so cool and dressed in his Sunday best. Afterwards I took him home after the return into Manchester which was a 16 hour day for me. I was now nearly 34 years old and never in my life had Dad ever congratulated me on anything really - he would just smile. He was just always very quiet about things concerning school, university and my Army results just like Colonel Walter Walsh ex-FBI. As we got to the farm he turned and quietly said 'I am so very, very proud of you - if I may give a piece of small advice and I know you have worked so hard in your life to get here but I don't think this job is really you deep down, I hope I have not offended you'. He knew I was very close to someone over several years but she had recently got engaged to someone else. This had really upset me as she was a lovely girl. He also knew deep down I really wanted to complete my military service.

For me your heart has to be really in something. As otherwise, if your heart's not in the right place, your endeavours will not be fulfilled. If I have no passion I don't operate.

Mum and Dad were so very worried during the Iraq war and Northern Ireland and when I had finally signed off fully on 22nd November 2007 Dad was very happy deep down. He died on the farm after checking his sheep two weeks later on 5th December, just after we had gone to visit him and Mum with my pregnant wife as we wanted him to know he was to be a grandfather. He never met my son (or daughter) but he did feel my son in my wife's tummy. His smile that night was precious; he was like a little boy. Life is so very short and so precious which I only realised so very late on.

So what? Finish what you start. I was a year late finishing my degree due to taking a year out for Operation Raleigh however, I still completed it. Then there was the military mess around with the 'Appointer (disappointer)' and completing my commission would take an additional three years yet I did complete this. Later on in my business world the mission was to fight and take on the banks, courts and lawyers and get my businesses and my family's and investors' money back. This whole process has been ongoing for several years and will very possibly take several more years to sort. It takes incredible belief in yourself when battling the system and when even family and friends and investors disbelieve you or think you cannot do it. It can be a very lonely and scary place but people can and do win. Without passion in anything life is just dead. You have to have passion in spades to get anything you really desire and succeed.

'F… Business'

Boris Johnson

7

World Trade Centre Attack 9/11

I tendered my resignation with the airline at the 24 month point and made sure the new Royal Navy Appointer had all my paperwork in order. A few friends in the airline made a few comments but roughly two years later those same friends sent some very encouraging messages.

I went to Dartmouth for a week then I attended the so-called baby Staff Course at the Tri Service centre at Shrivenham which was well structured and well funded. It was fascinating meeting all three military services. My Overall Directing Staff was Commodore Tim Lawrence Royal Navy, Princess Anne's husband. Then it was Sea King helicopter training at RNAS Culdrose involving simulator work and then flying training with 848 NAS at RNAS Yeovilton. I was immediately posted to 845 NAS as a frontline pilot and flew to Cyprus on ex-Saif Sareea in Oman and to the United Arab Emirates in the Middle East and met up with the Royal Navy fleet that had sailed out. As we landed at Akrotiri the 9/11 World Trade Centre attacks had just taken place…

Over my military service, I have been deployed on so many missions, never knowing when we would come back. And this was such an occasion. I had a really great first 10 years, all on the front line ranging from Belize, Germany, the Falklands, Northern Ireland, Norway, USA and the Far East as an Army Commando. Now I was to be a Navy Commando in a very different world with Al Qaeda who would be very different from the IRA. Over several months we ended up in 17 different locations, ships, hotels and airfields throughout different countries in the Middle East. I got to know the 845 Squadron people very well and we got to know Sea King helicopter operations in the sand very well too. The engines, the blades, and the people were getting sand blasted every day especially during the sandstorms.

8

Operation Telic
Invading Iraq

Those friends at Flying Colours, JMC and Thomas Cook then started to send messages through and it became clear that we would likely invade Iraq. The messages were basically saying it was a big call to re-enlist. They knew my personality and were a bit envious in a nice way 'and by the way 'H', do come back alive', the usual banter. It meant a lot as I was still justifying my career choice. In the USA and the UK after 9/11 a lot of the nation had joined or re-joined up.

Training got very intense and we had 22 helicopters and 3,000 Royal Marine Commandos on the HMS Ocean Helicopter carrier plus every attachment known to man including some US Navy SEALs. 845 Squadron under Commander Jon 'P' was in good hands. What people do not realise is that training can often be more dangerous than the actual live operations. In business years later the friendly forces can be as deadly as enemy forces as you will see.

As the Royal Navy and RFA travelled to Cyprus and then on to Iraq we worked on the decks of HMS Illustrious and HMS Oceans. Once, in the Atlantic, I nearly ran out of fuel in a Lynx helicopter when the ship ended up in the wrong location. It was easily done at night in bad weather. I had seen crews who had to ditch in the sea as they had run out of fuel. In one instance a helicopter was in a low hover, about to ditch into the sea and was hit by a ship. We reached them ten minutes later and they were all still alive.

There were several instances where mid-air collisions were close. One night, near Cyprus, we had two separate packets of two aircraft almost fly through each other, missing each other by just feet (an aircraft packet, or formation, can be two or up to six aircraft flying two rotor spans apart - so they would be flying in very close proximity). It happens and it did to me eight times. I would say that even with the best military training in the world, only 80% of it prepares you for war. This is the Pareto Principle. And it works the same in business. You just have to find the extra 20%. Later in COVID-19 I would have to find another 200% in business.

After this we then sailed up to Iraq. We had a USMC (United States Marine Corps) young Major come to HMS Ocean and brief us on the Iraq invasion Cruise Missile trace. At this stage we all thought diplomacy would stop the war. His brief made you feel as if you were as small as a grain of sand in view of Cruise Missiles. His advice was 'gentlemen and ladies you will be invading Iraq'. We then had a tense stand-off period and helicopter crews disembarked to train in Kuwait. Flying around we saw concentrations of US troops which looked like they were right out of Hollywood. There were tank crews from Alabama to Ohio, Texas to New York State; they had just had their second Pearl Harbour - the world trade centre attack in 2001. You could smell it from the air and see it on the ground. Their entire military forces were just colossal and were now going to war. I felt very small but well trained. Then 24 hours later we invaded Iraq on 'D' day. My own helicopter slot was 'H' hour plus 7 (hours) in a full general war invading Iraq on the premise of WMD (Weapons of Mass Destruction).

I was very worried, very nervous and very excited in equal measure. When politicians send young soldiers to war I wish I could bottle up that 24 hours of intensity so they can feel, touch and smell it before making these big decisions on their Armies, Navies, Marines and Air Forces. For the record we felt that our decision on the intelligence about the WMD was right. Months later I would be transporting huge black bin bags of WMD evidence with a small Royal Marine Brigadier as personal security.

The 845 NAS mission was rightly concentrated on getting the Al Faw terminal secure and no one really knew what the war advance progress would be after. The first wave went off with six aircraft all taking off at once and then the aircraft carrier really ramped up the activity. It can take several weeks and even months to get the entire crew to work together effectively and efficiently and to ensure that the systems are all 100%. For example tasks like feeding 3,000 people to fighting fires to organising PT on deck to then ground running helicopters and then flying all 22 of them all before nightfall!

My crew Lieutenant Dave 'T' and Corporal Marty 'A' had trained fully for months now and we all stayed in dedicated crew teams and launched pretty much on time. A CH46 Sea Knight had crashed the night before killing everyone on board with Major 'W', a Royal Marine whom I knew from the Royal Marine Brigade Patrol Group. It was torched into the sand at speed. Flying fast in a machine at a low level certainly makes you think of the balance of success and failure. This can be the same as in business.

Another two Sea Kings then had a mid-air collision at sea fairly early on in the war. We then took our helicopter with its underslung load onshore. This was a 29 Commando artillery gun and it was very heavy - it almost shook the old Sea King to bits. We saw that the Marines had done very well and Iraqi Tanks were everywhere, noticeably with the top hatches all open where they had escaped quickly. This was a good sign of the quality of our military.

We carried POWs (Prisoners of War) and injured troops from both the UK and Iraq. Memorably we carried a Royal Marine with his bottom sticking up on a stretcher where he had grenade shrapnel but he still smiled away. I can still see his cheeky grin now - good lad. We took in the first Royal Marine group wearing our gas mask respirators, this made flying hard and sweaty work. I noted they all looked like really young kids. Eighteen years later I would be in South Wigan trying to stop the banks, courts and lawyers ripping my property and business up after 12 years of hard work. And me physically fighting off immature older teenagers on drugs carrying knives and machetes, playing the big hero on their council estate compared to these young Royal Marines who were similar in age.

Eventually we ended up in Basrah and effectively overran

Saddam Hussein's regime. Then it was 'hash and trash' to get all the equipment off the ships and resupply 40 and 42 Commandos moving North West from Al Faw. 'Hash and trash' means to offload the stores of ships, aircraft and carriers.

There were a lot of displaced people and POWs. I remember a lot of 'bedouin style' tents, Toyota pickup trucks and electric pylons everywhere in a dirty oily desert (Kuwait's desert next door is immaculate) plus a weird sinister black flags system which seemed all very tribal or possibly to do with 'dark' forces. There were broken guns, tanks, lorries and anti-aircraft warfare guns everywhere. We did carry rendition POWs and I remember the odd high value targets. I also remember a couple of individuals who looked really evil, grumpy and unhappy about being captured in a noisy smelly old helicopter. Later on in a subsequent tour I took on board two SAS chaps whose mission it was to pick up the actual commander who gassed 5,000 people in Halabja, Iraq. We had to drop them in the middle of nowhere, near the Iraq/ Iranian border.

I remember one man - on his own he was a weapon of mass destruction. His look of pure evil I can still picture now and smell and touch it. I lost 34 colleagues in my 'average' service. 18 years later, I had a development building with 34 rooms in their memory, finished, which the bank ripped off me. This was one of the main reasons for this book - to name and shame the banks, courts, lawyers and councils.

On a more positive note over the years I was lucky enough with my Commando Sea King crews to rescue and keep technically alive 56 injured or dying soldiers by taking them to the field hospitals. Some sadly died later or had huge life changing injuries.

The IRT Rescue Sea King rescue and POW system was very good and everyone ensured total respect for all passengers, including the terrorists and POWs. Carrying the injured in your helicopter or POWs is always a very humbling, quiet and very serious business. There is a lot written about rendition and mistreatment of POWs or terrorists but we always treated everyone exactly the same and very carefully with no variation or maltreatment whatsoever. This is the Geneva Convention law (rendition is the process to hand from one international agency to another). We would always debrief as a three helicopter crew afterwards, especially with the door gunner or aircrewman who took the brunt of the mess and trauma. I helped develop a blood sheet with the engineers to make sure body fluids did not leak into the electrics in the Sea King. Adapt as in business.

Then it was all over and I was posted to my sister Commando Sea King Squadron 846. I was flown out almost straight away which was really odd after the intensity of it all and just 24 hours later I was having a beer at home.

So what? A mission in life is everything, and discipline and systems are needed in both the military and in business. During COVID-19 people struggled without a framework. I personally struggled a bit after military service in the late 90s and was very lonely and really bored after the intensity of military service.

Even when in situations of extreme distress and damage have that faith that the mission can be completed. Just do it and get on with it. There will be mess and damage and failure but this can always be cleared up later if you achieve what you set out to do. Don't ever accept larger organisations and corporate bullies who run you over as an individual. It is just not right and you must stand up for yourself every time even if you are on your own, which you will be.

9

Back to Back Tours in Iraq, Beirut and Afghanistan

846 Squadron then settled into a battle rhythm supporting Operation Telic helicopter operations in Iraq. It was four months on and then seven weeks back in the UK on a continual cycle - back to back for several years. In many ways the tours after the war were even more dangerous than the war itself as the various tribes would just release ammunition at each other willy nilly. At night, 0.50 guns would be shot randomly at helicopters, which when looking through night vision goggles, looked like large milk bottles coming at you. In between we had to fit in ship deployments in Norway and the UK and also tasking and jungle deployments. This was all between 2003-2007 and it was in 2007 that I finished my commission and moved on.

After Northern Ireland the UK military commitment to both Iraq and Afghanistan was immense and we had a whole military generation definitely well over deployed, but I liked the pace. The UK public attention to the casualties and the repatriation shifted markedly and I felt that society started to have a renewed respect for the military much like the USA did after 9/11. I enjoyed serving on the frontline immensely but the prospect of working in a typical non-operational location or an HQ with all the bureaucracy filled me with dread. I was not interested in this side of the military.

The adage was that if you could survive Norway Arctic training you could fight, survive and fly anywhere in the world as the techniques for landing in snow were exactly the same as landing in sand. The snow and sand obscures vision and blinds and many of the 400 crashes in Iraq and Afghanistan will have this on their crash reports. Also in Iraq sandstorms, called Haboobs, can come in at night. They are very hard to see if you are facing a dark background with night vision goggles. Once at night in a formation of four aircraft three of us managed to find vehicles in the desert to land next to but the fourth had to go back to the carrier. He missed a vehicle by about 30 seconds due to a sandstorm coming in, it can be that quick. Whether a snow storm or a sand storm, it is the same. In the Royal Navy and Royal Marine Commandos there are only about ten people in the world who would be fully in-date and current who could brief and lead these types of missions and also fly whether in the desert, the jungle, the arctic and in both war and on terrorist operations. I was one of them, purely by consistently being on the frontline and in the 'arena'. As in business later, damage and lawyers can catch you out so very quickly as could the enemy and the weather.

In the Arctic there were rules about degrees celsius

minus temperatures. You could be in the field and operate helicopters up to minus 26°C; minus 18°C was the troop's limit for lung damage when running. If the temperature was at the helicopter's limit the gearboxes had to be kept heated 24/7 or they would simply shatter. I loved the extremes and the pushing of man and machine to the limits. The training would then move into the 3 Commando Brigade main winter exercise which included landing craft and shipping. It would amaze me resupplying the Mountain Leaders and the Special Boat Service troops in the middle of nowhere in the mountains, then seeing local Norwegian mums and dads with two small kids telemark skiing! They were so at ease with the environment as if they were just walking down a high street.

Then in between the back to back Iraq tours you had to keep your training up to date: jungle, arctic, shipping, fitness, weapons, combat survival and still support on tasks in the UK. It was very busy.

During this time my flight was exceptionally lucky to pick up a jungle training support exercise in Western Rhumba in Ghana, central West Africa with an SBS (Special Boat Service) Officer Major 'F' overseeing the Exercise Brigade Patrol Troop and Mountain Leader jungle training (the flight is the pilots engineers and commandos - small teams). On the ship, RFA Olna, I had 60 troops and three Sea Kings which were serviceable and able to fly the whole two months of the trip. This included sailing down to Ghana, operating in the jungle and then returning to the UK. I volunteered the whole Sea King detachment, all 60 of us, to do the first three nights of survival training. One night a mechanic got bitten by a huge snake and was taken to hospital. After he was checked and given the all clear he was back in the jungle the following day.

On the return to the UK I asked the ship's captain to get us onto the zero longitude and latitude not far offshore from Ghana, just so I could say I had been to the centre of the earth! We also said a few words over the site of the Battle of Trafalgar between Cadiz and the Strait of Gibraltar on the return. I still miss the ability of doing unusual things in unusual places with normal average people in exceptional circumstances. And I also miss the ability to be part of history and not be a bystander as we all were through COVID-19. Take the chances when you can in life as you only get one go. Go, ask, seek as in business.

The Iraq tours came and went with the summer months which were so punishing on the crews due to the extreme temperatures. We had special medical teams assessing the Sea King crews flying in 65°C plus cockpit temperatures with a mix of ambient and engine jet pipe temperatures recirculating into the aircraft. The troops on the ground with bergans (army rucksacks) and kit were just sweating it out too. Crews had huge weight losses averaging 20kg. We carried embassy staff, scientists, lawyers, politicians, media and pop groups and HMCG (Her Majesty's Consul General) staff.

From the AAC days in Northern Ireland, Lynx 'Bullbow' the helicopter camera surveillance system code, named at the time 'Broad Sabre' on Sea King, was brought into force together with our VIP, IRT and general resupply duties. It was busy and varied but more so for the Aircraft Captain. One night, a US F18 jet came flying into the Basrah base airspace, not realising we had helicopters on surveillance at very high altitude (hence we wore parachutes). He just missed a helicopter at high altitude and then missed another helicopter on the lower level by just 500 feet, then went right through my aircraft position missing us by 100 feet - right in front of our cockpit! We sent the codeword for a near collision which is 'Airprox' (or a near miss) to air traffic control. What a muppet!

On another night of flying we caught terrorists firing rockets into Basrah airfield. We were at a very high level so we could not engage immediately, my two Apache gunships on call were off station to the East and the C130 gunship 'Puff the Magic Dragon' was not suitable in urban areas anyway. Over the whole night we tracked the two escaping car borne teams and captured the whole group of 10 plus terrorists. We ordered the 3,000 troops on the ground into town and told them where to go to capture the terrorists. They captured the weapons, their phones, computers and vital intelligence, etc. This had major implications later on for terrorist network intelligence and I nearly got sacked for not opening fire. Battle and business can both be harsh places. Working smart not hard should also be a mantra in business.

About that same period of back to back tours of duty in Iraq, we were on duty as the Immediate Response Team IRT or so-called 'crash out' rescue aircraft when two SAS soldiers were captured by terrorists when their car broke down. We were the first on the scene in 12 minutes. Then followed eighteen hours of flying, both day and night and all the aircraft and crew, the 3,000 divisional troops and the troops on the ground worked together to save them. This was just such an amazing focus. Five helicopter commendations were awarded for just doing our 'average' job. We all refused to have our photos taken for command as we wanted to keep quiet in the background. Both troopers and CO of 22 SAS came to the squadron lines the next day to thank us all. 'Bravo Zulu'. Well done team. Exceptional teamwork again.

We did all sorts of unusual things from taking Generals down to Kuwait and bringing high level VIPs back. Once a UK Special Forces General wanted to get to Kuwait as he had lost his Range Rover in Basra airport because of the fog! In the end, using a bit of airline procedures on arrival, we eventually found his party and took them to Kuwait which was also fog bound. This happened occasionally as the south east winds would bring in moisture. It was very, very tight but he was massively impressed by the Sea King effort. Tri-service rivalry between the Army, the Navy, the Marines and the RAF was always present and tribal as it is in sport and as detachment commanders you had to fight your corner and make HQ aware of your capabilities. In Kuwait we then had to shut down due to the fog for half the day. I knew the 125 meter fog limits for the Civair jet flight from taking off from my airline days, so this meant that the General's flight could take off - which he duly did. Such details and knowledge are important in both the military and business.

Sometimes we got to go out to the ships in the Gulf or take a vicar or a bishop to a leper colony where the kids would throw stones at the helicopter. Those vicars and bishops were brave men! The US Army Corps of Engineers (their version of the Sappers) and British Sappers had us go and inspect hundreds of miles of electricity pylons half way up to the country towards Baghdad. Terrorists were blowing them up so that they could sell the copper on the black market. Red, amber and green from memory indicated 'all blown up', 'some still standing' and 'some with the cables'. Even a 'Fat Sapper' could cope with that lot. It was all OK until the USA team on board lost count and had to go back to the last village to start again. We were flying very low at 300 ft. to read the pylon numbers and at a slow 50 knots so we had to be careful with anti-aircraft gunfire near Al Kurna. This town was in fact the mighty Garden of Eden where the Tigris and Euphrates rivers met. Getting shot down inspecting pylons was not going to be engraved on my grave stone! It was a huge relief after all the 16 months over six tours of air raid sirens to be finally on the RAF Tristar and taking my body armour off at 10,000 ft. altitude. This was their rule for wearing body armour in an RAF aircraft and it was a bit like leaving Northern Ireland, you do your duty and move on.

In my last year or so of my service I had two unexpected detachments. There was Op Highbrow in Beirut to rescue diplomatic staff due to Hezbollah terrorist activity and then TF 142 in Afghanistan as a stand-in Operations Officer to support a 'specialist' unit visit to set up helicopters for them.

We were in Beirut during mid-summer 2007. The 846 Squadron Boss, Commander Mario 'C', heard a rumour that the UK needed an evacuation helicopter force for diplomatic staff in Beirut. We set off and were ready for action in 48 hours from Cyprus as our HQ flew with Civair to set up the airbridge. The general route was central France, Sardinia, Rome, Sicily, Corfu and then on down to Cyprus. It was during the summer holidays and it was obvious to everyone in Europe the UK diplomatic clearances and flight plans were too slow to be received or were ignored by everyone. We took it in turns to lead the six aircraft and I led the southern France, Sardinia, Rome, Sicily airspace route diverting to Practica Di Mare to the south of Rome and no one knew throughout the whole journey knew who we were. We just kept saying 'we are a rescue mission of six helicopters to Beirut with 35 souls on board' which seemed to do the trick. There were military helicopters and jets from all nations, strewn across Europe broken down, obviously all trying to evacuate their own missions from Beirut.

The Squadron HQ did their job really well and we settled in very quickly. The airbridge from memory and my log book showed that it was about a 65 minute flight. It was a route into the north and a route out to the south something like 1,500 ft. in 'feet dry' (over land) and 1,000 ft. out 'feet wet' (over water). The main issue was not just Hezbollah shelling in town (Hezbollah is the Lebanese Shia Islamist political party and militant group) but also Israeli warships, although on our side, wanting to shoot us down. You had to be very careful when using transponder squawk codes and paying heed to the time zones for code changes, frequencies and war ship call signs. 'Blue on blues' (relating to an attack made by one's own side that accidentally harms one's own forces) do occasionally occur due to poor communication and the fog of war. We took 'specialist security troops' in and 'diplomatic staff' out. The diplomatic staff could be dressed in everything from evening suits to beach wear, basically in whatever clothing they had on at the time of being rescued, just as long as they were free with what they could carry. We had some very funny sights back in Cyprus as they got off the aircraft kissing the ground with relief. Some of our team were allowed access to the U2 spy plane detachment who hosted us and I really liked the Budweiser can of beer traditionally given on landing. Small things.

We did the same recovery route with some judicious use of resorts and taking four days via Cannes which when we got there was *shut* for the holiday so we stayed in Monaco for the night. The next day we had to get the three Sea Kings out quickly in front of Roman Abramnovich's Boeing 767 in Cannes. The bizarre thing was that the military carnet payment cards did not work too well in France so I had to use my own credit card to refuel the three Sea King helicopters at the one airfield open in all of France. To refuel three Sea King helicopters is not cheap! We only just made it back to RNAS Yeovilton, our home base in the UK. I filled in all the paperwork on route and left the expenses sheet on the boss's desk. Apparently in four days we had spent the whole Squadron Travel and Subsistence budget for the entire year. Some accountant managed to sort this out with a government official with bigger pockets and put it on the operational Beirut Highbrow budget. Flexibility is the key word all the time in military aviation and later in business.

The last evolution before leaving service was standing in for the 846 Operations Officer and helping set up the recce and set up for Sea Kings to work in Afghanistan with both the Green Army and Special Forces. It was all a far cry from the first few days in Iraq with old four tonne trucks and old Landrovers. It was now more a scene from a James Bond film, the vast spending increase between Iraq and Afghanistan was obvious to see from Apache gun-ships to the latest armoured trucks, mine proofed to a degree, to UAV (Unmanned Aerial Vehicle) drones and huge civilian contractors with huge Antonov AN225 aircraft. It was like Fred Karno's Circus, all very varied and very interesting.

I now walked away with my business done in Bastion and Kandahar. We flew back over the Red Desert where we were accompanied by two body bags containing two camera crewmen from a Combat Camera Team filming from a Chinook when it was shot down. One was Canadian and the other was from the UK. The 30 minute journey had all 20 passengers staring at the bodies. This was very sobering and made you realise the fragility of human life.

I had achieved my mission. I now wanted to get into property development, create small businesses and maybe help rebuild the UK in a way, hopefully using my military skills. Would it be more hazardous than the military? It would certainly be a much lonelier, scarier and a more damaging place than any of the four wars I had been involved with.

Now to the main part of the book. I wanted the 18 years to date to contextualise the 12 years in business, the war on COVID-19 and the damage caused by the bank funding being pulled. Would my farming background mindset and military experiences help me?

So what? Now we move on to the horrific business stories which are the main part of the book. The military background could help in the exceptional times leading up to COVID-19 and the new post COVID-19 world.

The military covenant is a key cornerstone for me by doing the right thing for my own integrity, clearing my name and restarting effectively from the bottom. Rebuilding my businesses and paying my team back in full are my priorities even if the authorities, courts and lawyers hinder, block or delay this through their fee structures and *their* agenda. Their agenda has nothing whatsoever to do with my business values, it seems to be all about what they can earn out of the situation. In summary, the threats and damages in war and operations teach you in life to expect the unexpected. If people and corporations want to really damage you, they bloody well will. You just have to fight back. Unlike in the military no one else will do this, you are on your own - very much on your own. I felt later that as soon as there is any real hardship, people, associates and businesses will show their true colours and flee the 'ship'. What you have to do is to launch the life rafts and go after those you want back and those who show their true loyalty once you have given them the real facts. Some you will leave in the water. We never, ever left a trooper on the ground or on the battlefield alive or wounded. Respect is earned not given.

Falklands Swimming Pool 1991. 90 men, five months, 3 Troop. We have yet to swim in it.

3 Troop 8 Squadron 22 Engineer Regiment. Staff Sergeant Kev 'E' and Recce Sergeant Mick 'W' and the best troops in the world – Sappers. Stonehenge was the regimental Silver.

2003 Iraq Al Faw oil terminal 40 and 42 Commando raid. We stopped Saddam blowing it up. Green Berets BZ.

tish soldier with head and
ablaze flees his flaming
ior and baying Iraqi mob

*SAS rescue mission.
Our team brought
in the medics by
helicopter. 3,000
troops. Five
commendations that
day. An 'average' day.*

*Iraq - My unit
completed six tours
plus the invasion tour.
Duty totalling 16
months on that base.
We slept between
breeze blocks.*

Lt Cdr Hatchard
19 Nov - 17 Jan 07
78 x rockets

*Ghana jungle support
to Royal Marines.
So called 'Junglies'
and Junglie cunning.*

Iraq invasion and tanks destroyed. Humbling carrying POWs, injured soldiers and WMD papers.

Seeking firing anti-aircraft missile flares. Helicopter Warfare Officers kept us safe. Royal Navy Fleet Air Arm's best.

Media press embedded on the 2003 Iraq invasion. They reported fairly.

Helicopter crashes do occur - safe here. 400 crashes in Iraq and Afghanistan 2001-2007.

Norway arctic ice breaking drills.

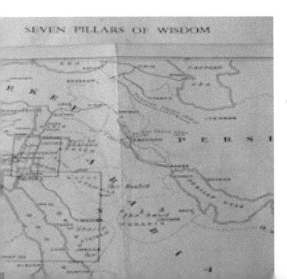

T.E Lawrence of Arabia in the red boxes in the 1920s. We were to the East in the 2000s and the Long Range Desert Group to the West in the 1940s. 100 years of Deserts and War in that one area of the world. 7 Pillars of Wisdom. Life going in full circles. Maybe there will be peace in the region one day.

Typical life-saving helicopter mission. He survived – my teams kept 56 alive on similar missions. Just doing our job. The wounded are just exceptional people. No booing or throwing cups here.

Brigadier Bagnold the LRDG* patron for expedition Sahara 87 - bottom right Long Range Desert Group*.

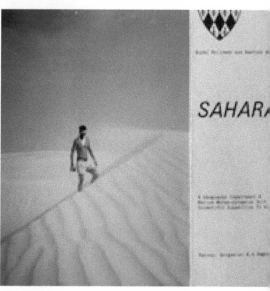

Sapper Army Divers helicopter dropping - Northern Ireland 1992.

Having a cuppa on the farm with Mum and Dad over from Northern Ireland. The AAC - another superb team.

Painting of HMS Ocean 2003 Iraq Army Navy Club. The buyer of 123 Bradshawgate in 2020 was a reputable Iraqi businessman.

Beirut evacuation Op Highbrow. This shot was the harbour complex. The UK diplomatic staff were very relieved.

Boeing 757 cockpit 'the office'.

Flying Colours airframe 'A' – which would eventually become Thomas Cook airlines before RBS refused their loan and they went into liquidation. Another ruined business. A very sad day.

The Priory Church of St Mary and St Cuthbert, Bolton Abbey

My father was true Yorkshire Grit. His eulogy - a very tough man. He taught me quietness, strength, hard work and to keep fighting.

*Getting ready for
Commando Training.
3.06 hours and
would still struggle
on the course.*

*The family we had
a crocodile as a pet
according to my
daughter and the
badges are hearts
- the mind of an
innocent child.*

*Operation Raleigh
Borneo. Some
would summit Mt
Kinabalu four times.
Superb people and
leaders all doing
great things in life.*

Diver helicopter drop training in the Falklands 1991.

*RE Sapper diver training.
Kit varied Kirby Morgan
to AGA to standard
'Awkward' code for
crash out the divers!*

*'...when I see defeat in the eyes of my
countrymen in your eyes right now....
we need to be reminded who we truly are....
we will not give up or give in...
do not tell me it cannot be done'.*

Franklyn Delano Roosevelt

10

Giving Back

I could have left the military and gone back to the airlines. What I did not want was to go back to being a shift worker, to be on standby and to have no control of my routine again. From my time at Flying Colours I did not want to start moving around airlines and damage my seniority with a difference of £60,000 per annum on which cockpit seat you occupied, left or right. I thoroughly respect all pilots and cabin crew in the industry and really enjoy flying now as a passenger. Deep down I really wanted to build something, a business or whatever that was 'mine' and start from nothing. Developing property and building SMEs seemed to be the route to do that. How difficult could it be after my career to date?

First I had to bury my father then help Mum prepare the tenanted farm to sell all the lorries, the tractors, the tools, the animals and the farm machinery. The farm sale was set up and was very well organised with all the barns set out for smaller items and the fields arranged with the tractors, lorry items and machinery. Food and drinks all ran out as we had over 500 farmers all turn up. It was frenetic. Everything went for crazy prices and the next day there was nothing left, just empty silence after 42 years of farming, family life and now sad emptiness. I took away a cow's milking kit, a milk churn and a shotgun as small keepsakes from the farm that had shaped me as a boy into a young man. Years later the bank even took the gun off me hence the 'suicide watch'.

Watching Mum hand back the farm keys really upset me. I remember to this day, for some reason, feeling looked down on by the lawyer who was present. I walked around the whole farm whilst the paperwork and keys were being returned. I remembered all the places I played as a child, the barns where the calves and lambs were born, the years of milking in the shippens, the bigger barns where we fixed tractors and lorries, the drains and dry stone work, the rabbits and moles, the lambing, calving and harvest celebrations with some cider and picnics amongst the hay when all completed. It was just farming life, the vitality of it all was now absolutely dead and completely gone.

I still have a dry stone wall headstone to keep for myself of where Dad fell and died. A family photo of me has my shadow of where he fell. If you are going to go then this was a good way to go. He had just checked his 'flock of sheep' overlooking the beautiful Bolton Abbey then passed away from a heart attack, a 'myocardial infarction' was entered on his death certificate. Mum at the time for some reason was worried and had gone to look for him and she gave him mouth to mouth for 45 minutes whilst the Yorkshire Air Ambulance came to assist but it was too late. We sent them a donation later. Ironically these were pilots trying daily to save lives. This was a full circle again. I felt really happy to be a simple farmer's son and a military serviceman. You felt as if you had really lived a proper life to the fullest, a life not spent just tapping away on a computer and texting on a phone all day long. I met Jeremy Clarkson in Iraq in October 2005 and at the time of writing I can see why his series called 'Clarkson's Farm' has been so popular. We had a farm in the family 200 years previous which was lost by marriage and now we had lost another tenanted farm through Dad passing. I just wanted to be a property and business owner and maybe one day get my own small farm and land.

Working with Mum preparing the farm items for sale had given me an opportunity to be close to her again. This closeness made up for my being away for so long and we spoke about some of the heart-breaking stories such as Dad having to help the Ministry shoot the whole cow herd during the BSE crisis. My parents had built up the whole herd over 30 years on the bloodlines. Mum was distraught as the cows were in calf and Mum's 'babies' were shot as well by the Ministry. Dad, who was a very hard man, never cried but had a tear that day. Being away on the frontline had insulated me from the challenges like BSE and the paperwork and ministerial regulations. Eventually this had all made making money on a 45 acre hill sheep farm impossible and it was the lorry work that filled in the shortfall. I helped Mum with the funeral arrangements and we gave Dad a simple send off with an appropriate and close knit community eulogy. My wife was very upset and hugely saddened as she was very close to him. But there was good during this time too, my son was born and I thoroughly enjoyed spending time with him and settling down to family life. I enjoyed having the space to enjoy something for myself for a change and it was the first time in a very long time.

At around that time I heard an advert on the car radio about an education programme based on Robert Kiyosaki's 'Rich Dad Poor Dad' brand which included amongst other things, property investing. That very weekend I attended one of their three day events and signed up for their advanced programme with a friendly guy called Mark Dalton. I was mentored by Mark initially and then was mentored by a chap called Sean Thomson. The advanced programme cost £17,988 and was structured over two years. It was expensive but it seemed the education and mentoring I was getting included good content. For my investment area I found a location 227 miles from my Dorset home, a blue-collar ex-coalfield town called Wigan.

I wanted to give back. There was a Lancaster bomber pilot Leonard Cheshire who left the RAF after WWII and created Cheshire Homes. So with Bradford Grammar School and my military service behind me I wanted to build something up after seeing all the destruction and damage in war zones. And to use the military strap line, I wanted to be a 'force for good' in business and 'rebuild Great Britain' with Hatchard Homes. My aim was to buy up brownfield sites, purchase empty buildings, refurbish and develop, refinance and then rent them out - it seemed an obvious way to fill that gap. I had left the military on 22nd November 2007 and it was just at this time that the recession had started. Life is about timing. At the age of 43 I had been insulated from the real world and from what really went on in business. It seemed that this was my chance to go ahead and build a proper group of businesses.

I also eventually wanted to coach and mentor business and property owners while using my military experience. I wanted to teach and give back. I was never one for training in a classroom and I wanted to be in the real world and teach the practical side. Not in a pretend theory world or third hand from someone else's hard work and property examples, I wanted to be real, to be a real investor and a real tangible developer. I had seen so much destruction so now I wanted to build and house families and businesses.

Another main driving factor for me for starting my own business was that Mum was effectively kicked off the farm after building it up for 42 years. We had all put so much work into the farm and had improved it hugely such as refurbishing the physical buildings and putting in drainage systems. Much of it was done by hand and it all simply went back to the landlord. It then dawned on me that it was OK building a business but I did not want to be a worker or a manager, I wanted to be the actual owner.

So what? I wanted to be the owner and have 'income generating assets' based on sensible borrowing with Bank of England base rates at 0.1% APR. Throughout my business career I have labelled the different times; the recession phase, the austerity phase, the compliance phase, the regulation phase, the Brexit phase and the COVID-19 phase. Looking back and in hindsight, throughout these 12 years, the finance would just become more and more restricted.

'Dad never attached much importance
to praise or sought it.
His typical comment at such times was,
'I was just one who was at that place and time
to do a job as well as I could.'

Walter Walsh (ex-FBI)

11

Building The Foundations

From the 'Rich Dad Poor Dad' affiliated training and my mentors, Sean Thomson and Mark Dalton, I paralleled the theory training over 16 months whilst at the same time actually developing terraced houses and completing refurbishments in tandem so as to match the theory with the real world. I have always been a realist. I was living on a camp bed in a northern ex-coal field town developing two to three bedroom brick terraced houses starting with 18 West Avenue and finishing with 2 May Street and 16 Findley Street. You never forget the house numbers. 18 West Avenue was an ex-drugs den and a three bed home built for Belgium refugees after WWI. I received the keys in January 2009 and started with a camp bed, an army sleeping bag, some porridge, some tea and my blue stove. I arranged to meet my local letting agent on site and we put a team of trades people together. Some tradesmen turned up on day one to begin work when it was minus 5°C in January with no heating. One tradesman complained that there was a drug addict who was sleeping rough upstairs but when this person came down he introduced himself as the owner.

My family came up on site but as it was so cold they just stayed for 20 minutes with my boy wrapped up and then went back to the hotel. I then bought 16 terraces in 16 months and finished all the refurbishments in 16 months exactly. This was with no heat whatsoever, just a bucket and toilet. I lived on site in all of the houses and helped the tradesmen do them up fully to as near to brand new as we could get. I would go swimming to use the showers and eat at McDonalds to warm up.

We had just bought a home in Dorset from a good Royal Navy friend. This was the same person whom I had met back in the Ireland days. I re-mortgaged our home, used my military pension and sold off anything not needed. I used the funds to buy and refurbish each small terrace house, which I then refinanced. At this time the UK was going through recession and starting to go through the period of George Osbourne's austerity phase as 2007 was the peak of the house prices then. Our challenge in 2009 was to buy houses at their true value. As a rule these were empty, smelly and run down but the owners still thought of them at achieving peak prices. We bought the first ones at roughly £53,000 and six months later we were getting the same houses at £38,000-£42,000 - these prices made the numbers better.

I had a simple refurbishment plan which meant completely stripping out each property. This included completely replastering and incorporating a full damp proof course from floor to about navel height which was the gravity reach of water soaking up the wall. Then it progressed to completely new electrical rewiring, gas central heating including new radiators and then a new bathroom and kitchen. All 16 houses needed a full damp proof course and half of them needed their roofs completely replacing. Once I started doing additional work such as taking windows out it became a big deal.

At one time when a roof had to come off, the basics of buildings became more apparent. To reroof a house you basically have to remove the slates, store them, and then replace the damaged ones. The battens and the strips of wood would then be removed and the membrane underneath would then be replaced with new membrane and fresh batten strips. You often see this on your streets. The membrane, not the tiles, is the waterproofing. The tiles are just used for protection from the rain, the hail and weathering cover as well as offering protection from birds. Reroofing needs scaffolding so it takes longer and the scaffolding adds more to the cost. Half of the houses we refurbished needed the windows replaced. Sometimes we kept the mahogany frames and weatherproofed yearly or replaced or added PVC windows where needed. PVC windows and doors of either white or dark or light wood effect have 10 year guarantees.

A full refurbishment would take six to nine weeks depending on whether a light, medium or heavy refurbishment is required. Prices twelve years later have changed with raw material prices and the cost of trades labour rising dramatically. At the time of writing, post COVID-19 late 2021, light refurbishing would be £6,000-£8,000, a medium refurbishment would be £11,000 and a full refurbishment would be £19,000 plus. The size of the house would also make the costs vary. Most two to three bedroom terraces vary from 850 sq. ft. to 1,100 sq. ft. The variation would then add 10-15% of costs if it was a larger unit. This was basic maths. You would start upstairs and we would do a roof check immediately. Often roof leaks are just simply caused by inadequate lead flashing around chimneys and possibly simple gutter leaks.

The problem for lettings and estate agents is that ladders seem to be an issue and scaffolding is expensive hence why so much roof property maintenance is never done well, if at all, by maintenance teams. This is purely simple laziness. Often properties with musty carpets or dog or animal mess, heavy smoking and drugs smelled foul but once the carpets had been removed and windows left open you would find the smells went quickly. This was important when sleeping on a camp bed on the floor. Properties lived in by heavy smokers amazed me. When a painting was removed from a white gloss or magnolia wall or a fitting was removed, you could see the nicotine stains. These are really awful to see, and I thought at the time 'I am glad that is not in my lungs!'

My business model was effectively a £40,000 purchase and a £20,000 refurbishment including professional fees and the GDV (Gross Development Value) would be an end value of approximately £80,000. As a general rule you would get a slightly higher end value if refinancing than a sale. If working on an industry refinance of 75% LTV (loan to value) or a basic ¾ loan, most buy-to-let property investors would have an 'interest only mortgage'. On your home you would typically have a repayment mortgage (capital plus interest). Commercially this would theoretically be capital and interest. So at 3-4% APR on your mortgage, your two to three bed buy-to-let would cash flow around £150-£200 net per calendar month. This would be all around the UK north of a line drawn from Bristol to Norfolk and outside the major cities. Here I am trying to explain the scenario of how the initial start of the property investing industry works. Later people often progress to HMO's (houses of multiple occupation) with anything from four to eight beds and 10 beds plus. These would involve bigger numbers with often larger cash flow or maybe they would move to the Airbnb model. This Airbnb model and the HMO hybrid means more returns but also demands more management time. With Airbnb you are essentially running a mini hotel.

Commercial investing is a different beast. And this all changed for the worst as you can see from the media articles supplied. Generally speaking we would sell a few units per annum to soak up small capital gains allowances and would make about £15,000 profit. So ideally I had to work out my hours of work to see if it was a profitable use of time. Here you would look at ROI (return on investment) but more importantly ROTI (return on time invested). Here is a key business education. If you as an SME, property investor or one to two person business owner begin to do 100 hour weeks and then run out of time then questions should be asked whether the monetary reward you are getting is worth your time invested. Delegation and ability are such important aspects to master especially when lazy or unreliable people come into the equation. People often say, especially in the post COVID-19 environment, that people can be so difficult to manage. Note to self, it was never ever the case in the military, people were its main asset. Later in 2021 the UK had over a million jobs available after effectively 18 months of a pandemic and still many had no work. With the UK furlough system in place politicians were having to issue work visas to bring lorry drivers, fruit pickers and care home assistants from abroad. That seems odd to me and just plain wrong. Or is it me?

The small developing process eventually became systemised. One main point is that tradesmen and others are not really bothered about your business. They would get paid on a Friday, often in cash. If being paid a day rate as opposed to a job rate they will take breaks all day long. Once on a set job rate they will work properly. I was often doing a lot of people's work for them if they were on a day rate and many of them would take you for a ride all day long. However, sometimes complex projects on some phases of development could only be done on a day rate so that had to be factored in.

Giving and serving in the military are good traits. In property and business you give an inch and I got raped and was for several years by various people. This is a strong term but it definitely was an unpleasant process. You don't see TV programmes about cowboy builders for nothing. It is because in a country of 66 million people regardless of location, tradesmen can and will be unprofessional. The good ones stick out a mile and are busy for a reason and will rarely advertise. It is nice when you see people wanting to build and improve life for people and do a good job. On the other side profit often comes first before any form of professionalism.

Professional investors cannot waste time with unreliable poor tradesmen. They need workers who turn up and do what they are being paid for. It is amazing how many plasterers, joiners, bathroom fitters and electricians cannot do their trade. Turning up on time, doing the job properly, invoicing and keeping things tidy seem to be so difficult for so many workers in the UK. Mobile phones really slow people down and major developers ban them for safety and productivity reasons. I have had good people and I can see why the Polish, for example, have such a great hard work ethic reputation. Without being ageist, be careful of much older tradesmen. They might have great experience but are often poor on administration and computers and can often start to take shortcuts and get lazy. The tradesmen you want to find are slightly younger hungry guys who are wanting success. As a business owner or property investor, everyone makes money from your delays. The lawyers, architects, builders, lettings agents, estate agents and planners all benefit. You plan to be on time and your profit is based on that as time is money. That helicopter will ditch in the sea if you or the ship is late. I know I have been hovering over them when this occurred.

The buy-to-let process worked well. The model was modified slightly as we had more corporate coloured carpets which weren't too dark, so we used these in both the properties for sale and the properties for rent. They looked much nicer. The properties looked more 'corporate' and less like social housing. And so we refurbished the properties for sale and the properties for rent exactly the same, just in case we had to sell quickly. And it is just as well we did this as we had to sell quickly in 2020 and 2021 due to the banks pulling in the finance and crash selling all my assets.

We used the same Howdens kitchens which were already assembled therefore saving days of labour making up cheap B&Q flat pack units. I also employed a basic model called the '£2k concept' for the small developments on seven main broad activities involving plaster, gas and heating, electrics, wood, carpets, painting and miscellaneous. I calculated that these broad activities would cost no more than £2,000. In total, that would be £14,000 plus, noting the light, medium or heavy refurbishment approach and the size of the building which would put another 25% on top in some cases. Pricing for window works, roofing, landscaping for drives and courtyards would be added on top of this. I always ensured a great curb appeal to finish. You can see the final results in the photo section.

This last property section of the book I realise can be a bit back to basics for the reader but is vital to understand how the property industry works before we progress up to the larger developments.

There were plenty of odd and often bizarre and funny stories that went on in the industry. I did a viewing once in a Wigan terrace described as a three bed and knowing the street you would get a feel for certain building and layout types. I assumed on this unit at 7 Selwyn Street that the third bedroom was in the loft. Once we got into the property it was very obvious that it was very small. It had a lounge and kitchen on the ground floor with the stairs up the middle onto the landing. As I turned onto the landing I then had to climb into a bath and then get out the other side to get to the three bedrooms. The owner had put the bath and toilet onto the landing and left the sink in one of the bedrooms. We bought it cheaply and turned it back into a two bed property putting the bath back where it belonged.

Another funny story occurred when I was mentoring clients in the Midlands where we viewed a student HMO at about 3 p.m. The two clients with me were both smartly dressed and the estate agent (he might have been the letting agent) wore a tie and jacket. The agent knocked on the door knowing that any of the students might be studying at home. There was no reply and so we entered. We were inspecting the kitchen when a student in his dressing gown, who had clearly just got up, joined us. It was very funny to watch him follow us around, eating a bowl of cereal and watching proceedings, then at the end saying his father might want to buy the house and would try to gazump my clients. What a muppet.

Another time I was with clients near Leeds. The agent was a bit vacant so I jumped in and led the clients around a very poor and dilapidated property. You do have to be careful as I have seen people fall through floors and stairs before. In this particular house there was an M16 machine gun and a hand grenade. I think we called the Ammunition Technical Officer. I asked the agent who said it had been on the market for six months and he had done 30 viewings of the property in that condition. Machine guns and grenades should be on the battlefield last time I looked. What did I know?

I had another viewing near Solihull in the Midlands. Often agents are not the most responsive to provide customer service, usually the estate agent or letting agent would open the door, throw the particulars at you and then spend 10-15 minutes on their mobile phone in the garden. The Purple Bricks model is to have key holders who just open the front door but often do not know anything of the layout or anything about the house. I realise their business model is to keep commission fees down. When I think about sales in the UK, I do like the American style where they can be bothered to give great service and *try* to sell the building. So many times I think if it was my property selling for £100,000, £200,000 or £350,000 that the agent I had given it to sell might *try and actually earn their commission.* The selling, buying and lettings industry as well as builders needs to grow up and adjust to the 21st century.

On a basic buy-to-let property an extra £1,000 of value earned might only be 1.5% of the deal with their commission and at 1% that has to be worth the extra sell. On larger units, the people and mobile technology are great but Donald Trump's 'Art of The Deal' book shows that the art of business is actually doing business face to face, that is where they are getting results. Even today I always accompany the RICS survey valuers on my valuations which they often hate. Later you will see an appalling example of laziness from a RICS valuer. Some sellers too who market their properties themselves or have the keys can be so arrogant by offering restricted viewing times and having other off putting habits. In the UK it still amazes me that there are such a huge number of empty buildings with so many homeless people throughout the country. On that line of thought in the UK we seem to value accommodation for bats as more important than housing for human beings. You might think that is odd but stop and think for a moment, it is absolutely true. I also get very annoyed seeing ex-soldiers sleeping rough on the streets. Later we will look at why the high streets in the UK are becoming vacant of shops and other businesses.

So what? After refurbishing 16 terraced properties I was starting to want to progress to bigger units and regenerate more. There is an industry publication called YPN, Your Property Network which has about 130,000 subscribers and there are many thousands of small businesses of so called 'Mom and Pop' one or two people enterprises such as MOT stations, hairdressers, hot food take outs, taxi drivers, stall holders, lorry drivers and the like with cash who will all do a couple of buys-to-lets. This is a cottage industry which supplies property, not the big industry boys who dig up green field sites. Take a walk in a city or town and see all the empty buildings, both the ground and upper floors, that could be done up to house people if only the banks would lend.

In my local town there are currently 100 out of 476 business premises that are shuttered up and closed. If you could get access to funds of say £20,000 on each unit with the UK base rate of 0.1% APR and did the shop up and the small two bed flat above, think what would that do for society. If say 50 units were done up that would house 50-100 people with council tax at over £100,000 per annum and provide 5,000 footfall visitors weekly in 50 shops generating £1 million of retail spending needing multi-storey car parking. Would that not be fantastic? If councils could be sensible and provide longer stay parking then families would come in to stay longer, shop and eat. I mention this here because like Wing Commander Leonard Cheshire, I wanted to regenerate and create communities unlike the banks, lawyers and courts damaging businesses during COVID-19 instead of showing pragmatic forbearance. You do not need the media excuse of Amazon online or COVID-19 to damage towns and city communities. The banks, courts and lawyers did this so very well themselves. Ask yourself why so many towns are so run down. There has to be another way.

'When everything seems to be going against you, remember that the airplane takes off against the wind, not with it'.

Henry Ford

12

Working with Investors

As I built up the terraces, the last property needed extra funds after I had exhausted my own so I used £40,000 investors' money on that unit. As we finished I started to attend property events called either PINs or PENS (Property Investors Network and Property Entrepreneurs Network). These were basically a network of property meetings usually based over a working day evening for a few hours. At one such event I saw a development opportunity at an ex-military airfield in Cornwall. This was at Travisker, St Eval which was an old RAF Shackleton airbase near Newquay airport and a group called Block and Estate and their builder subcontractor PIP from Hull had 118 ex-MOD married quarters to sell to investors. Interestingly each unit needed £75,000 per house, which Block and Estate would acquire bridging finance on and then need £40,000 per refurbishment. We had to find the £40,000 and this exactly matched the last block investor on the last terrace which fitted my plan well.

I went to my family and friends' network and on my initial assessment thought I could purchase eight units. I also had previous knowledge of the site as a good commando friend was posted there and so I knew the site's location. It was just eight miles from a fantastic beach in Cornwall. I popped down to do the military recce and had a good look round the area and the whole MQ (married quarter) site. Annington Homes had already started some of the houses and they were being refurbished to a reasonably good standard. I had a good look round the area and produced my own military style recce report including the market and local geographical area. One thing to note was that we were right at the start of the development. This represented a level of risk but the comparables i.e. other types of the semi-detached homes in the area were very good. Also, there was the attraction of Rick Stein, the celebrity chef, at nearby Padstow with some very desirable eating places and pubs nearby.

For me, the Travisker St Eval business model was to supply the holiday home market, local workers and provide a minimal amount of social housing to rent and then exit lend with a buy-to-let mortgage lender. The funds required would, in my estimation, be approximately £125,000-£130,000 with a potential £150,000 exit price so it had a sensible price or would work on a buy-to-let refinance. The developer, PIP, brought workers down from Hull which should have saved a lot in labour costs. It took some weeks to get the contracts, not helped by the fact that Block and Estate management team were based in Essex. Once I exchanged on my eight units (three were on Hudson Road and five were on Warwick Crescent), I then set about 'my' systems of what I had done on all my terraces. I stripped out all the copper which was a lot and from memory it was worth well over £2,000 at the time.

I managed to get this done just in time when the PIP, Block and Estate directors and management all turned up in suits with Bentleys, Ferraris and Lamborghinis which unnerved me a bit. I was filthy and wearing overalls having taken the last copper tank out of the very last terrace and was loading my 15 year old Honda Accord up to go to the scrap yard. They immediately came over and said I had to leave the site, that the investors had been waiting a long time to get going and what was I doing here anyway. I replied that I had exchanged and was stripping *my* copper out to pay for my fuel for the next four to five months. They called the insurance ticket and told me I had to leave to which I replied that I would but I wanted to know when I would get completion on my *eight* houses.

My old Honda had all the copper piping marks inside on the roof and it took several days to strip and load. I tried to hire local tradesmen to help me but they proved very unreliable. I sensed they were more interested in surfing than working. In fact I found throughout the whole development the whole atmosphere of the site and any local trades used was a holiday one. I spent a lot of time chivvying things up and I started to get more and more frustrated especially as I was the largest investor with eight units.

Block and Estate completed the legals on my first unit, one of the first three bed semi-detached homes. This was very late which was frustrating because their bridging loan was costing me extra each month to supplement *their* cash flow. We later found out they would delay specifically to make more money from bridging. Later in the book you will see the damage of how the UK financial system has restricted any small business or property developments since 2009 and over my 12 years of developing since the last recession. At the time of writing the UK base rate is 0.1% APR, the lowest cost of money in over 400 years. Bridging or unregulated lending as you will see, can and did go, north of 25% APR. Why then would the builder develop on time? The first three units on site were a difficult evolution for a supposedly good builder 'PIP' who had a supposed good reputation. PIP and as usual the main contractor on site was not a good leader. I was down there nearly every week or every two weeks, often after coaching and mentoring, or from Dorset to do a half day to then drive all the way to Wigan to oversee the properties there for my other work so I had long and tiring 90-100 hour weeks to see such slow progress.

The first house had a lot of snags and I felt it was an experimentation. I had my 'model' for the kitchens, the bathrooms and the garden area which included the erection of a wooden fence which I had an outside contractor to do. The extras were adding up and eventually I found a really nice couple on site who went back and did all the snagging and brought the units up to the standard I had expected from the original poor contractor. This eventually made eight great semi-detached homes despite the extra expenses to bring them up to the right standard. However, it was such a Herculean effort to do this, how many times have you paid for goods and services and gotten less than you asked for? And how many people reading this have had a builder come to their homes to do an extension, a loft conversion or improvement works, then have vowed never to use that builder again? The poor contractor builder business model works well for these operators who know full well that the client won't come back as a once only business unlike a restaurant or holiday supplier where you would go back. 'Check a Trader' is fine but I remember we used one in Dorset who had glowing returns and knew how the algorithms worked but who was not an accredited 'Gas Safe' (ex-Corgi) supplier. He would do the work but then used a ticketed supplier to sign the work off for him. This happens a lot so check them. Real business or fake.

I was getting annoyed now and was losing precious family time as my daughter was born during this. Six months later we had a cheap beach holiday nearby. I think we stayed with friends to keep costs down on site and all I remember is my daughter eating the beach sand. We still laugh about it now. It was a small piece of humour amongst a mounting sea of frustration, increasing anger and the belief I was working with a greedy team at Block and Estate and PIP with poor leaders and poor trades workers being treated badly by the 'Bentley boys' drivers. I vowed I would never take anything out of the business before the investors. To this day I have a very modest old car and would have to work 20-25 hours a week, even on family holidays, to cover shortfalls. I was effectively living off £44 per day from my military pension for the five to six days a week away from home. My money has always stayed in the business despite what people might say, as evidenced by my accountant returns. This experience was not my vision as I had had with the successful Falklands swimming pool team.

Then the major problem occurred with the second of the five houses as the site noticeably started to look more run down and now showed a complete lack of productivity. One of my

Army guys came down on site and saw his investment looking very run down which was not helped by a wet and dreary day. Even to this day I still complement his resilience. He ended up helping on the exit lending as the banks were starting to restrict and they restricted more from 2010-2012. More on this later. My last batch of five houses had been stripped out and the breeze block walls erected and internally plastered but we were approaching winter with all the door and window openings still open. The houses were completely wet inside and becoming a real mess so I wanted the properties weather proofed quickly but no one on site seemed bothered.

It then became clear in early 2012 that Block and Estate and PIP were stalling. I immediately called a meeting of both sets of directors and I had a small Army day rucksack with me which appeared full. Basically Philip 'B' who I had never liked, as well as the head of PIP, and the contractor main foreman plus Block and Estate had all run out of money and PIP had a skeleton crew effectively doing nothing. If it was me I would have sold the Bentleys, Ferraris and Lamborghinis and built the houses out and finished my mission. Unlike most of the other 118 building investors who had hardly ever been on site, I had been down there over 40 times in the year and I was becoming a real pain for them and rightly so. I had an advantage in that I knew the better tradesmen and some of the trades team leaders who I compared to great Army Corporals and Navy Killicks (Killick is slang for a Royal Navy sailor with the rank of leading seaman). I knew they could get things done and I knew the suppliers of kitchens, bathrooms and miscellaneous things needed to complete and finish each project.

They said they were waiting for funds. This might go on for another 12 months and would accrue even more bridging fees. Bridging or unregulated lending was a term I would over the years come to hate with a vengeance. Why pay up to 25% APR on penalty fees with the Bank of England base rates at 0.1% APR? I said to them that if they gave my first five houses full priority, not work on any other units and complete them all in five months (i.e. one per month), I said right here right now I have £50,000 in my rucksack which I will give to you. A deal was struck and I was to bring cash every Friday and I would personally check the progress on the cascade flow diagram with their own and my own foreman to double check. I wrote out a piece of A4 with one sheet stating as such with two copies double signed from memory. I then took the rucksack and drove off. The rucksack was full of newspapers...

Then I had to go and raise the extra £50,000 which I did the next week.

Even with this in place, I had to kick the teams on the next five semi-detached houses every week for five months plus every hour God sent. I also ensured that instead of them doing the same item of work on all five units, one after the other, they would do a single house to completion so I could then rent it and get finance in place. Each house had to be habitable to be mortgageable and get rents in to produce cash flow. The UK also at this time had a ridiculous six months' ownership rule, supposedly to stop mortgage fraud as the Council of Mortgage Lenders could not understand someone buying a run-down house, doing it up, then it being worth more than before. Bizarre. Compliance and regulation not only involved carbon dioxide and carbon monoxide monitors to fire regulations, it involved finance and the old Council of Mortgage Lenders now known as UK Finance. Basically the cancer was starting to spread as the articles in the photo section show, specifically the excellent articles by James Hurley at the Times, Andrew Verity at the BBC and Paul Keddy at the 'i' (newspaper). These media articles on their dates really show my property investing journey matching the restrictions with the base rate at 0.1% APR. I then realised just how archaic some sections were in the industry and the soon to be more onerous compliance and regulation phase after the austerity phase. Also I could see with growing uneasiness all the middle men taking their cut while you as the entrepreneur and business owner would endure long days, long nights and huge stress and would be at the end of the queue to take the final crumbs. By hook or by crook I got all eight units finished, painted, carpeted, the gardens fenced and fully completed expecting buy-to-let mortgages to be easily available.

One other issue was the site. Due to the mess, which inherently properties are in the ground phase, this was making the whole existing Married Quarters site, the so called 'patch', very run down and we were getting very bad ASBO issues. A local community action group headed by a lady called Sarah was making noises plus a neighbourhood watch group were muttering.

From my experience in Wigan I called the police after gunshots were fired into one of my windows and drug addicts were found smoking in abandoned buildings. The police were slow until I explained that 118 houses paying £100 per calendar month of council tax would add an extra £141,600 per annum into the council tax coffers. One hundred and eighteen houses x £100 per calendar month x 12 months of the year = £141,600. (In 12 years all my units have contributed £1,485,000 of council tax and business rates into the communities on empty buildings which are all now in active use). Sometimes I had to state the blindingly obvious to get anything done. Eventually the police patrols increased and the guns and drugs moved on. And as the police increased on the ground they eventually came good especially as every house was filled one by one which started to encourage community family spirit. This additionally created extra work, taxes and more business for the local supermarket and small coffee shop. 'Re-building Great Britain' and 'a Force for Good' was always in the forefront of my mind if no one else's. Northern Ireland, Iraq, Beirut, Afghanistan, Portsmouth, Wigan and Cornwall - all the same.

Back on the St Eval project, which was incredibly hard work, I thought the exit finance would be straightforward. Please do remember that I was also running another build site up in Wigan at the same time plus mentoring clients in London too for three days a week to keep on top of the bridging fees. Then we came to the exit lending on the site to get the funds, the investors paid off and to pay off the bridging. Eight mortgages on eight effectively brand-new semi-detached homes with now a supposed end value of £150,000 each with a queue of people renting at £650 per calendar month should have been a no brainer. As Top Gear used to say 'how difficult could it be?' In one word, difficult!

We came to the point where the dreaded RICS valuation surveys needed to be done. This was always a nervous time.

On the monopolies and mergers commission now the CMA (Competition and Markets Authority) you were with mortgage lenders who supposedly had a choice of panel RICS surveyors to value the units. Someone decided that with the military site, the anti-social behaviour orders, the lack of occupancy and a myriad of silly reasons, I could not get all eight units mortgaged and that we could only get five loans i.e. one on every other house. Bridging had already overrun and so now I had three units that I was unable to finance. In a discussion with one of my friends I asked him if he would 'mortgage host' for me so that if I gave him the funds and sorted the paperwork then we would get a mortgage in his name and then progress. And this is what we did. Due to the restrictions we ended up with about five different lenders as the build-up on terraces we were using each of the so-called 'life lines' up e.g, Natwest might do three mortgages, Virgin four, Godiva or Coventry three more, Birmingham Midshires two and Mortgage Express three mortgages as this was their limit. Acquiring the finance just took forever. To this day I still cannot get over lending criteria especially with the cost of money historically so utterly cheap. Today those houses are now worth £250,000 or £2 million together yet the banks had restricted their lending. Well done the banks. As the Prime Minister before office once famously quoted 'f... business'. The banks were in broad daylight.

Then the RICS surveyors started varying valuations by some £20,000 for absolutely identical buildings. Every one of those houses was *exactly* the same. What I started to do was that if I was on site as the host i.e. eight times on eight different inspection dates with each surveyor, once I had an optimistic valuation I would then have a hard copy and then show it to the other RICS surveyors acting for the banks and even helped the other investors on site. Common sense.

Later back in Wigan I tried this with great success on two projects, an ex-hotel and an ex-brewery. I helped others with their apartments and shops as the financiers later in 2015-2020 started to get unbelievably nervous about lending. This was because Professional Indemnity clauses were being asked from everyone from builders, foremen, investors, maintenance persons, quantity surveyors and architects. All of a sudden being the action man in business and trying to be a sector leader started to be not such a good trait. I think this finance issue started to be a problem after 2008/2009 but would gradually build up over 12 years. Paul Keddy from the newspaper, 'i', was very prescient in his article about lending becoming harder and harder. In 2021 post COVID-19 it clearly was to become totally unworkable when the banks, finance houses, bridging companies and pensions just pulled out finance on perfectly great businesses and would charge even more money along with the lawyers. Lawyers would typically charge between £300 to £500 per hour for that service. This went on for months and then Block and Estate went into administration to protect themselves.

In twelve years I have seen people go into administration, using puppet directors, just to make money. Those that do it do it to protect themselves and then move on elsewhere. Then the situation of going into forced administration on people and limited companies arises, where lenders will not allow forbearance and they put you into administration without any business appreciation whatsoever. You will see later how damaging, ruthless and vicious this process is. In Cornwall, Block and Estate had about £50,000 which was a fat lawyers' fee which never ever came back to us. Later on we would see how the equity of 11 terrace sales was almost eaten up in legal fees when the bridging company pulled on us. Their loans went to 17% and 27% APR, an increase of 45-75% with the Bank of England base rate at 0.1 % APR and the selfish lawyer made £50,000 on ONE building being forced to sell. One word - greed. This is now under government review and Parliamentary petition.

Also Block and Estate tried to allow a letting agency called Acorn run the site for the investors. In Wigan I had a letting agency housing approximately 300 tenants who had a sensible fee structure of 8% per calendar month plus VAT. This is sustainable as if the letting agent charged any less they would not be able to stay in business. Having this knowledge I knew that Acorn would be rubbish. The whole Block and Estate concept was an £18 million site project run as if it was a business consisting of just a few buy-to-lets. You need local people on site to manage with local tradesmen as they know the market, the foibles, the social housing, the welfare process, the Tenant Landlord Act and the holiday market as well as company-let contacts.

Even then they might not get it right so how anyone was expected to do this from 300 miles away in the north east was a complete joke. I again took matters into my own hands and eventually with all the houses now fenced, I had them rented at £650 per calendar month using a local letting agent and a husband and wife team actually on site to deal with the snags and to complete the finishing touch ups. The maintenance work for several years was very minimal although there can be issues with houses near the coast as the salt water content can travel up to 1,500 feet. Therefore, the properties would suffer from salt erosion in the brick and wood. This is the same for helicopter engines where we have to wash their engines at sea, otherwise they would corrode. Metal, wood and brick are all the same in that they all suffer. At St Eval we were generally OK as we were inland and higher up. The better the build the easier the maintenance downstream.

Occupancy ran pre-COVID-19 to about 98.5% annually on everything from the Cornwall homes, Portsmouth seaside apartments, Wigan terraces, and later hotel shops, warehouse pods and offices to churches and to kids' gymnasiums. The build maintenance and lettings side we had good control of, spanning over five geographical sites, over 300 miles apart. The main bugbear was the finance issues on completion of the projects and even sometimes years after having rented them out and with three year track record audited accounts. When would these restrictions ever stop?

The mortgage hosting with my army colleague was complex but we made it work. The sheer effort of funding was not easy and it seemed at this stage to be hardly worth the workload. From memory since 2009 the Bank of England base rate has been 0.75%, 0.5% and now sits at 0.1% APR. It seemed to me that the rate was falling yet again on the Assets and Liabilities sheet. The Assets part was being used as security in 2012-2013 and certainly 2015 but it was starting to prove more and more onerous. All of a sudden for me, the investors, the bridging, the building and maintenance, plus mentoring and coaching work meant longer and longer hours.

When I did a ROTI calculator on my personal hour rate I was getting less than my local garage owner working at less than his £46 per hour. He walked to work then went home at 5.00 p.m. working a 38 hour week and seeing his kids and having weekends off. I was living on £44 a day pension and working 100 hour weeks. As for the kids...

To tie off the investors in St Eval, Cornwall I reflect back on the commando squadrons with my flying and diving pay. I was earning about the same as a right hand seat pilot for an SFO Boeing 757 on about £65,000 per annum pre-tax. As a business owner now my pension was £44 a day, I was living off camp beds or staying in cheap apartments or houses costing £400 per calendar month, while running a modest car and eating very carefully and sensibly. Note that most 'at risk' troops on the ground will be fighting and being killed or injured with salaries of £25,000 - £65,000 per annum. This was a very sobering thought.

So what? Of note I seemed to be doing all this asset building of income generating assets which just seemed to me to be benefiting others. Something deep down in my gut started to work its way into my subconscious about the 'system' and the brokers and banks which is why Paul Keddy's later period article and its timings is such a superb piece of journalism. And so are the articles written by Andrew Verity at the BBC and James Hurley at the Times.

One last thought, I was also now fully engaged with an ex-hotel project back in Wigan and managing four other buy-to-lets in Gosport and one near Bristol at Portishead. At least for now St Eval in Cornwall was up and running. The terraces in Wigan had a GDV of £1,280,000, Cornwall had a GDV of

£1,240,000 plus and Portsmouth had a GDV of approximately £800,000. These were all set up in about four years and all were just about full and rented. This was getting busy and it meant more time away from home.

'Attitude is a little thing that makes a big difference. Success is not final, failure is not fatal, it is the courage to continue that counts. If you're going through hell, keep going. Everyone has his day, and some days last longer than others'.

Winston Churchill

13

'Jewel in the Crown': 123 Bradshawgate 2013-2014

Halfway through the Cornwall development I had been monitoring a large ex-hotel called the Lilford Hotel, built in 1876, address 123 Bradshawgate. It was an older building right in the town centre of Leigh, south of Wigan. I had just completed, what in my mind was, a good value Commercial Property Course and wanted to dip my toe into developing apartments, developing retail shops and regenerating town centres.

Historically, the building was owned by a very rich landowner called Baron Lilford who seemed to have come into money by marriage and through the Wars of the Roses in 1455-1487. The postcode is in Lancashire Red Rose not far from the White Rose border in Yorkshire hence the name of the series of Wars of the Roses. The red rose is the traditional symbol of Lancashire and a white heraldic rose is used more broadly as a symbol of Yorkshire.

In the past, people and certain cultures have often made huge profits and gains from economic crises or wars, from either fighting and stealing. We now have the more modern era where rich individuals or banks and institutions make money by pulling out finance and raping and pillaging individuals and stealing small businesses which you will see time and time again in the second half of this book. Again that unpleasant rape word arises for an increasingly unpleasant business. I had been to four wars and I was not about to let the fifth war of COVID-19 and the enemy financiers steal off me.

I mention this now so that this historical context might make sense of the drama of the continuing restricted finance from 2009 to 2013 and continuing through 2018 onwards, onto my personal 'war' on COVID-19 in 2020 and 2021. I was to treat this as a war and rightly so. People would just start to get self-serving and selfish and like a true war they would show their real colours. I found it amazing when I had spent years building up relationships, projects and teams and that it all ended in a smash and grab scenario and just became a desperate grasp for money. Doors shut and people turned their backs on me after years of my having paid people well. These ranged from letting agents, builders, tenants who turned and refused entry and our suppliers who did the same. I had agents UK wide from the London mentoring business who I had given a lot of referral work over the years. For this I received nothing, they too then turned their backs on me, even defaming me to clients. Business is a jungle and I had to get the Iraq body armour back on.

Either way the 123 Bradshawgate hotel cost £3,000 to build in 1876 and as you can see from the photos, it was a grand gothic style building over three floors. If you did an inflation calculator in 2020 it would value the building at exactly £900,000. More on this later as this is incredibly interesting in a historically and financially contextual way. Life yet again would go in circles. We found an 1877 original drinks list including champagne bottles at 3 shillings and 6 pence. It was amazing seeing paperwork with the original trademark looking like the Star of David. I still have the original. Like my father on the farm I gave away about 20 originals to various people I was working with to give them my 'Yorkshire' luck to help them. All through COVID-19 I heard from none of them. Some are gladly now appearing slowly. Property and investing is a long game.

The main challenges (or so I thought) were to do a mixed-use development i.e. eight apartments over three floors, seven retail units on the ground floor plus an extra underground ten garage style self-storage units and land for eight cars. It was to be my own 'aircraft carrier' with no wasted space whatsoever. It was a simple model. Buy, get planning, bring utilities in, develop, complete and then rent and refinance just the same as the terraces in Wigan and the buy-to-lets in Cornwall. These types of buildings are rarely owned by individuals. This was owned by two limited companies and the land across the road was owned by an individual. Therefore this meant three sets of negotiations and then arranging planning and a so-called delayed completion. This took a huge amount of coordination. Part of the negotiation was that I could put a 10% deposit down and delay the completion for 16 months to then reduce borrowing costs. Or so I thought.

After about four months of messing around I bought it

with a mixture of funds. Even though I felt very disjointed coming out of Cornwall, I made it happen. I was asking a lot of people for help and realised that in 2013-2014 many so called professionals just did not know how to conduct each step required. A lot of alleged property experts, especially on the internet, just have a presenter standing in front of someone else's hotel talking about commercial property. Like the military you are either in the frontline combat zone or not. Stop pretending and don't be a fake. In the military we used to call these fake people Walter Mittys.

We adjusted the planning as we wanted to use the self-storage to add revenue. This is how you value these buildings. Also we used the new SBRR (Small Business Rates Relief) system to make sure the shops were below rateable values with the Valuation Office Appraiser whose role includes calculating both council tax and business rates to ensure tenants did not pay rates. At the time of writing rates were approximately 48-52% of the rental values so this would save a normal type business such as hairdressers, tattoo parlours, cafes, coffee shops, etc. a huge amount of money. For example, something like a small shop would pay in the north west of the UK £110 per week or £476 per calendar month in rent so the SBRR would make savings of rates in the order of £2,856 per annum. I thought this was valuable and I thought it would encourage people to start renting. Noting at the time, a rough search showed 100 units out of 476 units on the main high street were empty with a very poor high street presence which was not helped by a drugs methadone issue right in the centre of town serving 200 drug addicts. But what about the other 60,000 occupants?

About this time in 2012-2014 the full effects of George Osbourne's austerity programme were being felt. I had agreed with this initially but like Brexit later it went on for far too long and then ran into the finance onerous compliance and regulation period. Now a financial cancer, unknown to me at the time, was now implanted in the initial phase fermenting as we started on 123 Bradshawgate.

By exchanging I had secured the building for just under £395,000. Soon after I started a very simple method of buying by price per square foot. I would assess the build costs, the fully developed gross development value, the Full Market Appraisal value (or the final done up value) all by square feet. This is based on a USA method and stops you overpaying on the front end of the deal. It is simple and it stops you from buying property too expensively at the start. You make money on the deal buying in, not when you sell.

Since I was waiting for the planning department we started unusually in the beer drays in the basement and built out 10 soundproofed and lockable self-storage units complete with a pump in case it flooded. It never has flooded in seven years as we are above the water table and not in a flood plain area. But this does make a huge difference on planning insurance and valuation purposes as well taking into account the distance from the local coal mine shafts sunk in the mid 1800s. Any reason for not lending, the finance houses will find it. The fact that locally 30,000 buildings have existed for over 100 years and were still standing is obviously ignored by lenders and surveyors.

I now mention the town of Leigh which was a key site during the Industrial Revolution. It was involved in cotton milling, coal mining and held many Industrial Revolution patents. It was in many ways the silicon valley of the world with the natural soft water flat land ideal for the canals and the best quality coal seams in the world in 1800-1900. Of note, the area still would be one of the best sites for shale gas mining in the 21st century. Life comes in circles again. One hundred and ten years later when I arrived in 2009 Leigh had a population of 40,000. It was very poor and run down with the local Right Honourable Andy Burnham as MP (now Manchester Metro Mayor). Andy Burnham was instrumental in the creation of the £85 million Olympic Leigh Sports Stadium and Leigh Sports Village with seating for 12,000. Twelve years later Leigh now boasts a £60 million canal marina development, two major hospitals with a value of £100 million, the Manchester guided busway with a value of £68 million, Tesco Cineworld with a value of £52 million, the current South Canal development with a value of £3 million and further funding of £20 million earmarked for 2022. The population is nearer 60,000 now and has a retail catchment area of 498,000. Andy Burnham opened many of my buildings. However, there was still no proper commercial lending. 'Why not?' I asked myself.

I mention this now as when I came into the area only the Leigh Sports Village main stadium, college and sports centre were up and running. I used to sleep on the camp bed in the terraces and when the carpet man turned up I would take everything out of the building such as the paint pots and tools and load them into my old Honda. As a treat I would go and stay at the Leigh Sports Village in the Park Inn for one night at £50 while the carpet fitter did all the carpets. The Park

Inn is now a Holiday Inn Express. I did this 16 times for 16 houses over 16 months and was the only person in the hotel being waited on by 36 staff. The hotel is now full every night and they have eighteen staff with room rates up to £80 a night. How the town and indeed the world has changed in twelve years and it changed even more so later during COVID-19.

A major problem with the 'Jewel in the Crown', 123 Bradshawgate were the RICS survey valuations at the end of the project. More on this later, first let's focus on the purchase. This was to be a commercial horror story that would start to unfold in 2015 but would only really manifest during COVID-19 with loans being pulled as well as including a legal minefield in terms of valuing properties. We also had an issue with one of the sellers of the limited companies because we arranged a delayed completion where his 90% funds would be paid to him right at the end and it was to be the same for the other limited company seller. All of this would happen when we had secured our magical exit loan of 75% LTV loan which would be a capital and interest loan. As before, how difficult could it be? You are about to find out.

The builder was a locally recommended one who was a good refurbisher of the terraces but this was a big project. The other builder had 30 years of bigger projects on his CV. Effectively they were doing the same job. The building was not yet set up with all its planning permissions in place and needed utilities brought in. We were only made fully aware of the utilities mid-way through. Additionally to this I had to set up supplier contracts locally including suppliers in Liverpool. This was not ideal. In its favour the building had had a lot of work done already in the roof works, the structure and the main underpinning which I assessed roughly at £125,000. In hindsight I had slightly overpaid for the building but not by much.

Three years later, I bought the building next door, 100 Lord Street. I paid £400,000 for 15,000 sq. ft. The idea here was to buy roughly at below £40 sq. ft, refurbish it with a cost of £20 sq. ft. and have a GDV end value or full market appraisal of £94 sq. ft. and maybe in time £100 sq. ft. The terrace model can still work at this bigger level. The difference on 100 Lord Street next door was that we increased the floor space by adding a complete new floor on the existing structure. This equated to an additional 33% of floor space. The subtle difference between the two developments was that one had structural work already done and the second didn't so it was a balance between the two asking which was the best approach on profit and keeping costs down. The issue with these complex brownfield sites is that the refurbishment works are very difficult to price up. Once we had a retail shop and a one or two bed apartment mocked up then that would be the model that we used on both 123 Bradshawgate and later 100 Lord Street.

Wigan Planners on the so-called charter were supposed to issue planning within six to eight weeks. I have found from experience that this always ended up at six to eight months. David Rawsthorne, whilst a great individual, in the council he struggled to get through the red tape and lack of staff through continued government cuts. Investor developers who are borrowing money at £500 plus a day cannot put up with this cost but planners are *generally* ignorant as they do not have these pressures. The UK planning system in Portsmouth,

Cornwall, Bristol and Wigan and in fact throughout the UK is not fit for purpose for the reasons above. In New Zealand you can exchange and complete in two days whereas in the UK it is six months minimum. Planning is the same creating such uneconomic delays. All the middle men get more money from delays which means that you as the investor just lose more and more money. In March 2021 in the UK 95,540 people were in temporary accommodation and 68,000 were listed as homeless out of 66,500,000 people. This is a national disgrace especially since many ex-servicemen and women are included in these figures. When I looked at this in the cold light of day we are in the 21st century and since people have lived in caves they have needed to be housed. We just seem as a country to have forgotten how to put people into buildings quickly, sensibly and cheaply in a way that benefits everyone and society. There is no systemised finance or banking for property and certainly commercial units, from my diary since 2015 onwards, which means that things are just getting worse and worse.

The 2013-2014 build was slow. Also the two project managers fell out and we had assaults logged with police and one walked off site. I suspect as he had his own big project he, I assumed, had worked out what money he needed and as soon as he had made the money he needed for his own project he walked off. This happened to me several times with tradesmen and foremen. Airlines might not have been glamorous but after Cornwall this was starting to get unprofessional and frankly very silly. People seemed to be taking me for a ride. I was taking all the risk and effectively doing the work of many people. I used to drive and do over 45,000 miles a year and wondered why motorway road workers were never onsite days at a time. Road works with no workers, an empty build site or a retail serviced shop unmanned will not get work or productivity done. Period.

I seemed to sense that the so-called 'Jewel in the Crown' was becoming a money pit. The contractor on site had recommended an architect who had apparently been a main member of the Royal Institute of British Architects. All I knew was that with my other business I was coaching and mentoring until Thursday night then driving up overnight to arrive at 01:00 a.m. on the Friday. This was every week or every second one and it meant that by Friday morning I had already done a 60 hour week. This allegedly professional architect would frequently be two hours late and sometimes he would not turn up at all. The only thing I got out of this man before he went bust was the ability to use a Meccano type metal framework to put more units in which I would use for the next two projects to great effect. I was getting annoyed with this cottage industry. I had moved into the Cornwall airfield with a £1,280,000 development and now on to this potential £1 million ex-hotel to get away from what I thought was a hard work cottage industry. However, things were getting worse, not better. I had to keep going.

My mother would come down and sometimes help clean up. My mother at age 70 could work harder than anyone on site. My father would have been furious with me and she voiced her opinion as such. Again, as in Cornwall, I was kicking people to get things done for things that they should have been doing and were being paid well for. We eventually got an apartment and one shop completed so Building Control, which was a *good* department at Wigan Council, would then say 'yes, good job' and then do a midpoint appraisal and an end of project appraisal for a final sign off. This process and the building control man worked well locally. I also noted at the time I was having to find more trades people to cover unreliable ones. I would have thought the contractor would have had the trades people and suppliers in hand and under control but I had to keep on top of this as well as do all the paperwork. All the contractor would supply was the wage bill on a scrap piece of paper or text at the end of the week. There were no audited accounts or anything. They never even filed accounts at Companies House.

About twelve months in I asked about the water and electrics and whether we had enough water and electric pressure and what the potential difference was which received blank stares from the team yet again. I had decided no gas was needed as it was seemingly more hassle and would add even more cost to the build and electric 'greener' systems were becoming more efficient. So I asked the main contractor to bring in new water supplies to which he said he did not know how to do this. He had been in the industry for about 35 years and yes, you guessed it, this created more workload for me.

Architects and builders can be as clueless as each other but the quality of build was good so I put it down to my teaching people which I was doing to both tradesmen and my mentoring and coaching students. I went to United Utilities for water and Electricity North West for electricity. I mention this now as the former is a monopoly in the north west and the latter is simply a cartel in the north west. This was yet another example of the Competition and Markets Authority again not doing their job. Effectively you pay in full three months in advance then they go to a subcontractor to do the trenching. Again here this was the most convoluted route and we had to bring both utilities from across the main high street road in two separate trenches at different times.

This meant that the project overran by four months whilst I was getting tenants in myself because the experienced builder had no idea how the utility tender process worked. The tradesmen who did come in to bring the utility supplies were very good and they certainly should have been because the electricity from memory was £23,000 and the water £17,000. Not cheap. Also on top the council wanted CIL/S106 payments as an extra stealth tax to pay for 'a children's playground' type approach plus they wanted business rates payable throughout which I declined as the property was uninhabitable. This went to nearly one year on tribunal and they pulled out the day before after hundreds of my workload emails. It would be the same five years later on 100 Lord Street next door.

On top of this we found the building to be in a conservation area and although we had nearly all new PVC windows on the dormers, the top floor and all on the first floor, the council said we had to now *replace* them *all* with antique mahogany. This would have been another £40,000. I was fast falling out with the council. I was now just a cash cow for tradesmen, contractors, architects and now a greedy council bearing in mind that the building had been a run-down pub and carpet warehouse which had all failed and given nothing back to the community for ten years. I was about to supply a 10,000 sq. ft. building back to the community with seven new shops and eight new apartments, 10 self-storage units as well as designated car parking with a rent roll of £82,500 a year all bringing in business rates for the council and new footfall. Over twelve years this was a project that would put £18,000 per annum of extra council tax and business rates back into Wigan to pay for schools and hospitals. I was now feeling that I was a punch bag and yet another cash cow for the Wigan locals. This might seem harsh but over twelve years we put £1,485,000 of funds back into the local community on empty buildings. We were now paying business rates and council tax. Later in 2021 I was to receive absolutely no support from them and even more taxation on top was being demanded. With the council it was seemingly now 'let's take as much money off this man as possible'.

There is always a silver lining in a cloud overhanging a sea of despair. After various calls to Wigan Council to try to overthrow their demand of replacing all the brand new windows they were adamant and threatened to put a stop to the building works. One of the joiners then found a crumpled up piece of paper jammed in the window casing. It was Wigan Council giving permission three or four years previously to put in PVC windows! That just saved £40,000 and three years later would save another £50,000 in the building next door which was also in the conservation area so we could also fit PVC windows there too. The tradesmen got a case of beer. When I approached the council they said they had no knowledge of this. I had gone into this commercial sector to be more professional. This was utterly unbelievable. More on this council later.

I remember the Falklands swimming pool where the whole

team wanted to work with overnight shifts for the mission to succeed fully. The rescue commendation I received in Iraq in 2005 (one of five issued that day) together with 3,000 UK troops were all pulled in as a team to finish the job in 24 hours and to save two SAS soldiers lives. I was now seeing why so many ex-military people get so frustrated and angry when they leave service to come across all the nonsense that I was experiencing. Later in the book as Brexit uncertainty and then COVID-19 set in, this approach from council, trades workers and indeed banks, the greed of the courts and lawyers would just get worse and worse. This was beginning to be the start of the terminal cancer setting in.

In my gut I was now starting to appreciate why high streets were dead or dying. I was coaching and mentoring firstly UK clients and then I moved to international clients based in London. The UK clients meant mentoring all round the UK from Cornwall to South Wales, London to Newcastle and also Wigan. I was seeing the high street decline all round the UK and it had nothing whatsoever to do with Amazon and the internet as being portrayed by the lesser informed press. It was caused by the banks starting not to lend, by bridging companies lending at loan shark rates of 27% APR and with such greedy councils taking more and more as well as builders unable to build with a systemised approach. The terraces seemed so much easier but I was on 123 Bradshawgate and soon to be 100 Lord Street developing 25 and 32 units in one go which had a productivity of time element of roughly one per month. Remember the 16 terraces in 16 months one per month? How different this was. Keep going 'H'.

The project overran time by 50% but it was now

completely finished and oddly for these types of projects and the run down town centre, at least at 'our' end the shops filled really, really quickly. This was probably aided by no business rates on the SBRR system, parking and effectively being brand new inside. Maybe at last I was onto something here. On commercial run-down units most commercial owners normally let the tenants do all the work themselves. We instead did all the work to bring them up to 'as new' and we also paid the FRI (Full Repairing and Insuring) and CAM (Common Area Maintenance) to increase our support to fill the buildings. The rent roll in full is how they supposedly get valued. In four months the whole building was 100% rented and eight apartments were paying council tax. The gross rents were £82,500 per annum, not a bad pension for someone and we achieved this in under two years.

I remember Mum coming down in early December and offering tea and mince pies in our show home which was the main corner unit and the main shop windows being fitted with prospective clients inside. It was freezing cold with Right Honourable Andy Burnham MP for Leigh and the Lady Mayor of Leigh in attendance. Interestingly Mayors serve just one year and are more senior to MPs which surprised me. Anyway, the Lady Mayor of Leigh seemed helpful and nice and I treated everyone with respect. Like the Sultan of Brunei years ago when we tried to 'sell' him the helicopters, we were always taught to host senior officers and VIP's in the same way and with courtesy.

Due to the contractor problem with bringing in the utility supplies and therefore having limited electric lighting, I had been to Wilco and bought small battery light packs to put into the toilets as they were pitch black and had all the doors wedged open. This worked. Even with all that, 75% of the building was signed up. Staging property is so very important and you don't need a 'show home' wasting more money at this level I would argue.

This seemed to be success at last which one would expect after such huge work and input and 'kicking' everyone to get it done. Two major items occurred when we completed the building bearing in mind that bringing in the water and electrics were four months late. However, that got sorted and we rented it out fully. We had to complete the delayed completion with the two limited companies and get commercial exit lending as soon as possible. I was to approach the two sellers once I had the exit lending remembering that now I had investors' money from Cornwall burning a hole in my pocket plus a large bridging loan which had gone to the extension rate from 12%-17% and 16%-27% APR due to the initial delays. This was thanks to the delayed building, delayed utilities, delayed planning, fraudulent seller and delayed exit lending from the banks that never fully materialised. It seemed that this was all happening yet again.

Now the first seller's legal documents were ready but then the second seller dropped a bombshell and said he had secondary loans on his eight apartment leases for another £160,000 and could not complete. What a total idiot and fraudster, Patrick Duckworth, we now have him paying £111 per calendar month, the balance will no doubt go to his estate on his death for us to get the remainder. Another bigger bombshell was that the broker who I was to do three supposed large deals with then declared that Shawbrook bank RICS surveys had down valued and now would not lend on the commercial shops but 'might' after six months - remembering I was now £800,000 into the unit. They had just valued the building at £225,000 with the controlled valuation by Shawbrook. RICS fraud in my mind. I will write that valuation again for the reader at £225,000 just in case you thought this was a typo. I immediately then paid for two extra surveys. The next two valuations came in at £295,000 and £495,000. Well done Hannah and Pettys based in Manchester, yet more unprofessional RICS surveyors. My Professional Indemnity would not cover that utter 'unprofessionalism' and refused to pay out.

I was now panicking. I had done our rent rolls based on an 8.5% capitalisation rate which meant my exit valuation or GDV should be approximately £950,000 remembering that my original business plan was £1 million which was not bad for my first commercial effort if the banks lent. Remember the inflation adjusted £3,000 in 1876 would now be £900,000. Then I did some research on Byron and Thomas based in Stockport, and found a really nice, jovial RICS surveyor ex-Commando called Leslie Byron who had an MBE for services to the Fire Service. He came in and over coffee I quickly supplied the full rent roll in 60 minutes. In seven days I had a valuation for £855,000 from Leslie which the broker and Shawbrook bank would then *not* accept. We had to then take the Shawbrook lending if only to get the 27% bridging finance off as soon as possible and then we had to find the £160,000 from the fraudulent seller's company. Bad to worse with the advice 'don't worry 'H' just keep renting for another six months and you can then get a further advance from Shawbrook'. I checked on my Professional Indemnity insurance clause and yet again in my insurance experience I was magically not covered. Over twelve years insurers would be a total waste of time remembering later in COVID-19 how many just refused to pay out or put immediate exclusion clauses in. This paying for goods and services that would not produce then became worse and worse during the Brexit negotiation period and it all came to a head with COVID-19. This sector might contest my comments. On one of the buildings I currently have 8,600 emails hence the 120 hour weeks spent dealing with this increasing type of utter unprofessionalism in commercial property lending, underwriting and building. Indeed in everything.

Also at this time I cast my eye over the bridging loan agreement noting the expensive exit clauses if it was cashed in early. More on this later. So now we had electricity and water, had paid the fraudulent seller, had a 'half' of a so-called commercial mortgage from Shawbrook and I did have full completion and freehold. In two to three months we had full occupancy at approximately £82,500 per annum in gross rents on a building I had valued with my own team at £855,000 and not the ridiculous Hannah and Petty RICS surveyors at £225,000, £295,000 and £495,000 end valuations. This was a massive difference. In any other industry this would simply be fraud. The building in 2018 would be valued at £925,000 with Sanderson Weatherall. If Hannah and Pettys read this I would like to see the letter 'P', for Professional, added on their RICS heading. Joking aside I also started to question why RICS were carrying a Royal Warrant with all this ridiculous undervaluation just in case Her Royal Majesty the Queen is reading this. 'Ma'am again sorry for crashing one of your helicopters'. The man who fell from a helicopter...

I felt that this banking and commercial valuation industry was starting to become a complete fraud. Later during COVID-19 in 2020 100 Lord Street was crash sold by Together Finance. In reality it was worth £1,900,000 but had a reserve price now set at £1,050,000 by lawyers Duff and Phelps. This meant we were adrift by £850,000! And the investors and the lawyers are calling it all a fraud! If I did not like some lawyers now, I would soon hate them as much as the courts and lenders. By the way, this auction was recorded on film. I mention this now on the trend to what was to happen later in Brexit and Covid eras. How would a reader like it if their own home when they came to sell it was valued at half of what they had paid for it? There had to be a better way. I had to keep trying and keep going as in Commando and Diver training. Operation 'Awkward' in military diver training is a pro-word to crash out the standby diver in emergencies to save a life (a pro-word is a code word in an emergency which is agreed on beforehand). Banks and lawyers were being awkward and they were hurting me financially.

At the six month point I went to Mark 'H', a finance broker, and said 'right, I would like to get the extra further advance now' only to be told that Shawbrook had changed their minds and now wanted a full three years proof of rents'. This was now a complete joke. I then went to Aldermore Bank although we still had restricted lending on the shops in terms of Loan to Value. I managed to get a small increase on lending noting now that through the onerous exit clause the broker received *another* £20,000 for exiting the contract which was about what he also 'earned' for setting the deal up in the first place to get Shawbrook out and Aldermore in. And here I thought the buy-to-let mortgages in Cornwall were unprofessional and a con...

You might think that the lending scenario up to this point was bad but in the next six years it was set to get worse and worse and downright ridiculous in terms of cost, security and workload. Of note, out of 345 so called UK banks and lending houses like Shawbrook, Aldermore, Amicus, Together Finance, Redwood and so forth include challenger outfits which do not operate out of high street premises. They were now telling me that due to my lack of corporate history and credit rating my lending had to be in individual names and with personal guarantees therefore meaning that we would have absolutely no protection. I remember saying to one of three main brokers I was using saying I should write an article about this to expose the industry in about 2016. His reply was 'I would not do that if I was you, 'H'.' I remember that reply really haunting me at the time. Something was not right.

So what? You can sense that now out of 345 lenders we were 'bottom feeding' on so-called lending demanding increasing levels of extra security with no protection and unarranged extension fees of 27% APR plus. Yet the Bank of England base rates were at 0.1% APR, the lowest lending rates in 400 years. In the photo section there are some really superb media articles that came out in 2020-2021 which, in hindsight, were building up to COVID-19.

After all this work, I would still have to work while on family holidays (which were few and far between). I tried to hide this additional work but it was difficult. It was OK trying to be a businessman and supposed entrepreneur with long hours as the finance repeatedly kept being restricted but it was eventually going to damage not only the individual but the family too. It was eventually bound to suffer past the point of no return. The sad thing is that in my gut I just started to realise that this financial cancer would be terminal. I just knew deep down.

No wonder later in early 2021 Mike Norcross the 'Out of Essex' TV star and property developer committed suicide. On his Coroner's report dated July 2021 in both the BBC and Mail articles it stated that all the increasing and onerous bridging, increased lending costs plus additional pensions, extra cars and other finance policies he was trying to raise more and more money for developing with more and more family home security on his loans, all which simply killed him in the end. I genuinely felt so sorry for him and his family as I read the report on the circumstances it sounded just like my financial situation. He had in January 2021 a £5.3 million asset base over three developments which were all unfinished. On my research for the book over twelve years, I eventually would have £7,950,000 *all completed* and all *fully rented* achieving £522,000 gross rents per annum and yet there was still no proper exit lending. Where would this all end? Blood on the hands of the financial houses was now becoming more and more public

'The world ain't all sunshine and rainbows. It is a very mean and nasty place. And I don't care how tough you are, it will beat you to your knees and keep you there if you let it. You, me, or nobody is gonna hit as hard as life. But it ain't about how hard you're hit, it's about how hard you can get hit and keep moving forward, how much you can take and keep moving forward. That's how winning is done'.

Mohammed Ali

14

New Builds: 2-4 Brown Street North 2014-2015

Towards the end of Bradshawgate you may remember we had a small parcel of land that one of the directors had sold me. It was then when I asked the builder to go and clear the land for parking for seven cars which I could rent to the ex-hotel tenants. He came back and said that he had found previous foundations and that I should check with Wigan Council. In my research the council flatly said no, there had never been any buildings there. However, I had some old mapping, as I was interested in history from school days, and I could clearly see some buildings on an old Land Registry chart (original Land Registry land titles are beautiful documents with old stamps and wax seals) but Wigan Council still said no. Then one day I was talking to an old motorcycle shop owner who had a photo of his premises clearly showing a terraced house on my land site which was demolished in the 1960s slum clearance programme. Do these councils not keep records? Wigan Council said no again and I threatened to go to the local Leigh Journal newspaper asking why we couldn't improve housing in the town centre and regenerate and improve and increase quality housing for families and local businesses. I was getting really fed up with the small minded attitude of the council despite all my efforts to help. They then relented at last. Gotcha Wigan and we got our planning which then took several months not the stipulated six to eight weeks. In a word, persistence won. I was at this stage moving from project to project and keeping investors' money rolling, working and moving. I needed to keep the momentum going but I was realising that financial restrictions on the eight houses in St Eval, Cornwall and more recently the complete faff with the mortgaging of 123 Bradshawgate, the so called 'Jewel in the Crown', was creating so much workload and delays and downright stress. I was saying to myself 'surely things cannot get any harder?' The rest of the town was slowly developing but the town centre itself wasn't, but surely it would come. It had to, didn't it?

I was at this stage happy to parallel projects as long as people worked hard and kept work going and shared my vision. I eventually found a new builder (my other builder was busy on another project discussed below) who quoted for a new build to produce a large two bed flat over two small shops with a rear car parking space. Then unexpectedly, stage right, a Jewish hairdresser next door objected with a Party Wall Act obstruction action wanting, you guessed it, even more money. This was starting to get boring. It seemed that I was going around town with a big sign on my forehead saying 'take more money off this man'. With the same architect as

123 Bradshawgate we looked instead at a 'no compensation scheme' where we would sort a backyard area out plus an access point and make good any mess and build a wall and a gate. It was rejected but then accepted for some reason. Interestingly the Party Wall Act was not completed by lawyers but in this case two separate architects were involved. More on this later.

I had done my numbers based on the square footage. The land effectively was zero cost (the cost was born on the 123 Bradshawgate) and the build quote for a medium quality build was £126,500. This was a bit high by about 10% for a 1,360 ft. unit over two floors but my GDV end build valuation, based on a capitalisation rate of 8.5%, was ok at £141,846 achieving a £12,000 per annum gross rent. To value commercial property supposedly you take the gross/net rent divided by the 8.5% capitalisation rate (it varies in the UK, area to area, and on a smaller scale, zone to zone). Noting as they were all effectively new, the maintenance would be negligible on three year commercial leases as there would be no voids. So apart from the cost of the insurance there would be very little outgoings or so called MOE (monthly operating expenses). With a stronger rent the value would come up to £150,000 for a 75% LTV loan which would leave in about £14,000 so not bad for a new build first go attempt. Also I wanted a new build under my belt for my CV so I could coach and mentor properly having got that t-shirt. I did not want to do any coaching and mentoring unless I had actually completed a new build in the 'arena' and actually done it. Military rules.

Once we had planning permission, despite inclement weather, the build went ahead with very little disruption apart from the annoying hairdresser who was just one of life's 'odd' people. The hairdresser was a very nervous man who appeared on the site every day moaning about the noise and mess and prophetically the builder said 'he will be trouble'. In fact the builder, our architect, the hairdresser and the council would all be problems and would cause me more financial damage and extra expense. The council would occur some five years later. It was proving to be a greedy industry with greedy people with no team work – a real pattern was forming. Property was starting to become very hard work and unpleasant. It did not need to be like this.

Half way through the build, my architect decided to bankrupt himself so I simply asked the other architect Paul Baines who was good and who was acting for the hairdresser on the Party Wall Application to help me complete. I was told this is not normally done but I simply said why not. He was local, he knew the project inside out and that is how we finished the project. You have to cut through the BS as the so-called experts will just keep billing you again and again and again. I just wanted it done and to get on with people. The ghost of the Falklands swimming pool was on my right shoulder asking why does it have to keep being like this all the time?

Six months later when the building was finished, the builder never really bothered with any snagging but the quality was ok and so we did the snagging ourselves. We were yet again doing a lot of work for other people who were getting paid for it.

Throughout this time the cancer was spreading and later on occurred in four ways. The builder in a large future project locked us out, then there was a Party Wall Act claim which the builder refused to use his insurance for and he was also stealing supplies from the site. The builder then instigated a smear defamation campaign and we had assault charges with the police on his team wanting bigger bonuses. He was one of life's big bullies. More on this later.

On the subject of bullies, later on, bullying from two lawyers sadly had an effect on one of my team. He was a friend who walked out after 12 years citing the incident and the other parties' actions on my phone by text. I was really saddened that the bullying had had an effect on the associated businesses. He was to die six months later. This was very sad and totally premature in my mind and it was yet another very dark day. People who know me say that I just keep giving whilst others just take. If the latter is the mantra of success I would rather save soldiers' lives on the battlefield and be a real success and not be in a business harming people, businesses and property.

Through the book I go back to the military and forward to COVID-19 to keep giving context. Some five years later we were forced to sell due to a bridging company pulling out *immediately* on COVID-19 setting in and we had to sell 2-4 Brown Street, the new build. Then magically Wigan Council demanded from absolutely nowhere the dreaded extra tax called CIL/ S106 which is a mixture of Community Infrastructure Levy where so-called 'rich developers' pay more for projects to help the council and also an S106 to provide for more affordable housing. Great for the 'big boys' with deep pockets. *Five years* later this extra convenient bill was for an extra £12,000 plus. When you factored in the actual sales price, the legals, the conveyancing and agents' fees we had now made no money whatsoever. Well done Wigan Council and at the time of writing we are in dispute over this et al. I could either roll over or unusually for me, get quite angry. It was coming across as continuous financial greed at every single corner. I had created income generating assets and was now being a target for extra money at every corner I turned. Why?

So what? If you think this was bad, the hairdresser (he could have been a Martian for all I cared) then declared for damages against two of my companies. Remember, we had paid all the legal fees and had done all of the extra work at my cost. Throughout this Jazz Hairdressing would frequently ring Wigan Council complaining about *my* commercial bins that were being fly tipped by lazy locals in the town centre. Remember there were no bins at all before I came to town on any of my housing sites which now had them. I was now personally being threatened by the Wigan Refuse Department with department head Sean 'G' issuing £5,000 pest control fines. That hairdresser was not a very nice man and was also one of life's greedy people. He filed against one of my companies as the builder was ignoring calls and emails.

Then the hairdresser tried to damage another of my companies. When I checked over 200 separate insurance items with my insurer that I had with them over 12 years, magically there had been a lapse in policy for *just three months* and yes, you guessed it, the claim fell in the lapse date period and so it was declared not valid. This was sinister yet again and it is on file. I was now not covered on my Personal Indemnity! They filed claims against me and won over £36,000 plus expenses for a small external plastering mark. You could not write this in a Hollywood horror movie. I folded that company and I believe he is still chasing me now five years later. I have now called another regulatory body, the Legal Ombudsman, to investigate for fraud. This was six months of yet another property challenge and ironically it took place *after* the planning delays. This time however, the utilities were already on site and it was a perfectly straight forward build with the unit rented immediately – funny old life. It was easy to build and easy to rent, everything else just seemed farcical. Keep going 'Fat Sapper', onto the next project, surely things must get better...

'For warriors it is essential to keep the spirit of combat in mind twenty four hours a day, whether walking, standing still, sitting down, or reclining, never forgetting it'.

Code of The Samurai

15

Lease Options and Sublets: Platt Fold Street Warehouse 2014-2016

During the project of 2-4 Brown Street and 1 Back Queen Street I was approached by the owners of 100 Lord Street, which sat next to 123 Bradshawgate. (Note that postal addresses are dictated by street entry points which can and do make complications for everyone from MPAN (Meter Point Administration Number) designations for electricity, to delivery drivers and to post office workers but that is the system). 100 Lord Street was the location of the Burton Beer Brewing Company in the late 1800s and was now co-owned by Airflow Compressors Limited and the Ratcliffes Bicycle Company. I was approached approximately halfway through 2-4 Brown Street as Airflow Limited had just negotiated a move from the old dilapidated brewery, 100 Lord Street, to an equally dilapidated huge 36,000 square foot blue warehouse on Platt Fold Street, 150 metres down the road. Between the two parties we to'd and fro'd on the negotiation on 100 Lord Street. This was a hybrid of delayed completion and my doing some improvement works for the compressor business on Platt Fold Street. This took about 12 months so there would be an overlap of work on 2-4 Brown Street and Platt Fold Street and exchanging on 100 Lord Street. I could cope now with the volume of paperwork as St Eval, Cornwall was complete.

To summarise so as not to lose you, at this point in time, all eight units in Cornwall were now all completed, 2-4 Brown Street was ongoing and were on target and budget and we had an agreed purchase price for 100 Lord Street which was £400,000. This was subject to some planning considerations which we used to delay and control the purchase. We wanted to take over in about 12 months but both sellers were wanting to move as soon as possible. We told them to back off. At the same time we offered Airflow Compressors Limited about £20,000 of refurbished office values to match the 100 Lord Street deal to both sellers' parties. That bit worked well. The wife of one of the parties was an ex-lawyer and again was just a bit greedy. On more investigation into the warehouse on Platt Fold Street we realised that with failing businesses and failing management nearly the whole building was available, or certainly 80% of it. I had just completed the Commercial Training, Subletting and Lease Options Courses which seemed the way to control this particular deal. Also I was doing more and more mentoring to keep on top of costs. These were busy times.

Effectively with Platt Fold Street we started the works for Airflow Compressors Limited in one section of the unit at a time. There were eight sections in total. That took several months and then I approached the pension company owning Platt Fold Street to enquire about my taking a sublet on another section next door. I would later build a double storey 'show home' and 'pod offices' in this section. From memory this worked out at only an extra £100 per calendar month over my terrace show home for 4,500 sq. ft. of space and free parking, therefore it was so much space for the money. Then over the next 16 months we went from one end of the building to the far end developing over 90% of the whole unit and renting to an eclectic group of businesses ranging from compressors, to a plastics inventor, a Patek curry food machine maker, kids gyms, self-storage, skips companies, various pod office businesses and renting car parking. Pre-COVID-19 I had 98% occupancy rate of all my properties.

I eventually ended up with four, five year leases with a view to a potential option to purchase and exit lend onto a commercial mortgage at 75% LTV with pension holder approval. This was verbally discussed with a director for a date 2023 onwards from memory. This took quite a long time with my conveyancing lawyers and the pension lawyers, Berg and Co, who were very good to deal with. Of note, due to the bank damage later on, the lease option was voided with investor action against Hatchard Homes Limited. This action was not witnessed by serving lawyers and occurred whilst on a short family holiday. I found out on my return that a legal team was citing fraud. The investigation is now with the Legal Ombudsman, reference F092087. Wigan Council later in 2021 then declared the whole building planning and fire control regulations to be void. This was very odd as the rents and business rates had been paid for over 10 years before my time. In fact all the offices that we refurbished with £300,000 of investors' money were already constructed so any form of planning or fire regulations were extant, all except unit 6 which was brand new. This was Wigan Council again against business. They were not on my side and we would now have £300,000 of investors' money all potentially lost here. You have guessed it, the post COVID-19 Legal Ombudsman investigation referenced above is ongoing now. Still with me? Can you now really see how the financial cancer was trending? Just keep going 'H'.

I tried a variety of building tactics to tie in with potential tenants. Some parts of the building were very poor. For example the roof in places had collapsed and the transparent roof sections were very dirty and leaky so there was little natural light. This was slightly amusing as the unit it had belonged to previously was a roofing and ex-property company. We asked the landlord to get this sorted out. However, their subcontractor's work was not the best, it was minimal and often late. Some units had a mezzanine section and some of these offices were run down.

I fire filleted all eight units and then incorporated a paint scheme for the floor and walls of dark grey and magnolia. The window company we were using had gone bust so we bought £2,000 of normal white PVC windows for £100 which helped. In the far gable end we added extra windows for the pod offices which helped provide natural light and we added solar tubes and 'trade veluxes' for the roof sections. The idea was to keep energy conservation to efficient levels and this plan worked very well.

One simple practical conversion was that if we had half

a mezzanine section with stairs in the middle, we brought it forward and put the stairs to one side allowing vans to drive in and load out of the rain. Such simple ideas like that really worked. In another section we added more offices creating about 100% more use especially where they had double storeys. We also made judicious use of the toilet and kitchen areas. Where we had to be careful was the light industrial engineering alongside offices and the children's gym. All worked well for five years until COVID-19 when a dirty skip company really started to make a mess of the pod office section. There was constant conflict and tenants and their clients could be very rude and blunt. Mums and dads with kids would park anywhere and litter from kids using the gym was very problematic just as it was in the town generally.

I really liked the double mezzanine floor concept and also I liked the use of the day and night access and thankfully there would eventually be a solution for the littering issue. The kids would generally use the gym after 4 p.m. just after the majority of workers on the main warehouse had departed and the other light industry businesses had left. This was very lucky and it stopped a lot of conflict. This usage would start at 7 a.m. and would finish at around 11 p.m. This was just like the original American 7-11 shop concept of the same name. This worked out at 66% usage time-wise and the mezzanine double storage in 25% of the units so it was a great usage of space and time not unlike an aircraft carrier.

The issue was always the exit finance. As mentioned earlier I had put in over £300,000 into this unit. Again the banks and lending houses pulled out funds. This situation is currently with the Legal Ombudsman to re-ignite the original lease. I am happy to invest but not to have the warehouse pension company walk off with my investors' money especially with the council's position on fire regulations of the offices and planning and business rates. The lead director of the pension company, the managing letting agent and the council and administrators were all fully aware of the Legal Ombudsman investigation on where the rents were going. I did not mind working hard for my investors and making people money but I would not put up with this continuous ripping off by lenders causing me to 'Pull Pole'. ('Pull pole' is a term used in the Arctic with the Royal Marines where you break camp and the tent pole is the last thing to come down inside the tent, with the troops still inside, just in case the weather turns nasty. That way the tent can be erected immediately as frostbite and frostnip can occur so very quickly). This case is ongoing.

Positively speaking, the 32 units double storey self-storage was a great success. The van load area, the automatic lights and remote access for 24 hours were all very good and worked well. Generally the top floor was used by small domestic size unit users and the downstairs was used by the bigger commercial building stores where constant access was required. These units were generally a 'hands off' type of passive rental. The main bugbear after the parking was sorted was that the roof leaked.

Considering that we had maybe 80 people using the building from parking and self-storage to pod offices and light industry, we only had one constant complaint and that came from the kids' gym. They were business owners, two girls who kept trying to lower their rent payments below the market rate for their own benefit. The question here is, who is in control, the owner or the tenant? The owners end up putting a lot of investment into these units and working hard for tenants to improve the site, to improve the building and getting all the tenant clients to work together providing utilities and parking to help everyone. An 'aircraft carrier' and its team are imperative for the whole operation to work. If people were like this on a 'carrier' there would be accidents and you just cannot afford to be selfish on board ship. These business owners were not 'good' people. That was the only real issue. Squeaking wheels get oiled.

Another factor on the Platt Fold Street warehouse and why I was really interested in it was that it backed onto the £68 million guided busway. Leigh was the stop/start town where the buses ran on concrete channel sections and the bus shortened travel times into Salford and Manchester. Additionally there was a very large car parking area. I planned the works on the basis that the busway would open on time. It did not do so. Then getting tenants in was difficult and slow.

I remember in Iraq there were central planners thinking they could convert a newly occupied country to become a western democracy overnight. That was very naive indeed, the military does what it says on the tin very well normally but after the invasion, the rebuilding of a nation after is always so much more difficult. Look at what happened in Afghanistan, it had really appalling leadership once the military pulled out. Whether it be Basrah or Leigh or Wigan 150 years apart, we see the same differences. Leigh 150 years ago was the silicon valley of the world with coal, cotton and world class industrial revolution patents and yet today there was no commercial lending for regeneration. I should know from developing over 200 rental units.

Here I was in an ex-coalfield town and now after five years I was wanting things to happen quickly. It was clear now that this was not going to happen overnight. The busway opened nine months late as an example. Look at the ongoing delays of the UK HS2 fast rail system coming nearby to Leigh later this decade.

With regards to managing Platt Fold Street and finding commercial tenants, the lettings agency were on board with me helping them develop a sort of commercial and residential hybrid system. This was so they could manage both the commercial and residential tenants. The manager was on side but the owner less so with the day to day management. So yet again I had to keep giving more to make it work. I said to the owner to give me 12 months on the Platt Fold Street warehouse and that I would offer an extra 1% increase on his management fees and that he could walk away if the warehouse tenancies were not filled. If we did fill them then the management fee would reduce back to normal 8% plus VAT. Once the guided busway was completed their car park filled up immediately and then each unit we had also filled up immediately. It was amazing to watch and I won against the agent's bet.

As always I was asking a lot of people how to put it all together and I again realised I was having to use my initiative to get things done which was OK, it just took time and energy. One item of note was that using a residential agent to market commercial property without social media meant that the uptake was slow but it worked well for finding commercial agents on a finder fee basis. We went to 10 local commercial lettings agents with clients on their books who then for a finder fee would hand clients over to my team to manage. The biggest criticism was that the commercial agents never ever called back, almost to the point of them being arrogant. I was finding that the area was very slow to adapt to my 'let's just try anything or something approach'. It was very frustrating but I got there in the end.

Another aspect of my trying to be pragmatic in a town where it was all take and no give was the car parking. My mother used to say people would park their cars in the shops if they could. With the guided busway and the newly completed 123 Bradshawgate 'The Jewel in the Crown', we found that the Platt Fold Street warehouse was getting much busier. It was so busy that we were getting cars parked randomly all over the place and that they were not parked efficiently. I then found a really good professional road and tarmacadam painter specialist who painted 80 car park spaces including pedestrian walkways and restricted signs for only £1,500. The paint dried in 10 minutes! Sometimes I would not even haggle over prices where I thought it was amazing value and it certainly was here. He was simply a good tradesman to deal with. There are good people around you but you have to find the 10% not the 90% who will take from you continuously and deliver poor service. This is often the case in lower end building works.

We then found cars would park up properly and we could get three times more vehicles in. Some tenants had free spaces with their rental units and some tenants paid extra rent for caravans, taxis, buses and lorry parking spaces. People responded to the signage well. What I did find was that all letting agents I used over time could drop off in service like all humans and I was constantly 'bucking them up' every six months to provide the service. This happened many times, more so with the commercial agents where they tended to 'drift away' from day to day. This 'bucking up' worked actually quite well. I then instigated an extra warden to manage the building. He had a free office for his own business and was getting paid. His idea of management was to send photos of the bins overflowing and photos of car registrations. He wasn't proactive at all and this was very poor especially as I gave his company a considerable amount of work and a free office. Later as we approached into COVID-19 the letting agent and warden services, for the best part of 12 months, became increasingly poor and tenants on site started to leave. More on this management side later.

So what? Despite another Herculean effort to build out Platt Fold Street which was relatively straightforward yet was very difficult to cost up the job, I spent about £295,000-£300,000 on just over 30,000 plus sq. ft. of floor space. This was a spend of just under £10 per sq. ft, which was very reasonable remembering I had the four, five year leases on the whole building, not owned but I had the potential verbal option to purchase. The Legal Ombudsman now has this case too. The hybrid system on rentals, leases and car parking and getting more electricity proved to be a huge headache but once set up it proved to be very efficient.

Lastly, people get very nervous of Japanese Knotweed. There was a small infestation in one corner which we simply treated every early autumn three years in a row. Mortgage lenders were getting twitchy again. These people need to go on a military combat operation to get the concept of real risk! I was always so pragmatic and getting over obstacles for me it was always 'how can we do this?' yet for everyone else it was always 'how can we not'. Overall Platt Fold Street was a good project, it was straightforward and the lease sublet option worked well. It just needed coordination and a good letting agent willing to take it on.

As I said before the projects were all about lining up and coordinating between them. The difference with Platt Fold Street was that the sublet lease meant that no deposit had to be put down (which would have been upwards of £400,000). We just had to find the development costs. Eventually the rents were £5,300 plus VAT per calendar month and the rent roll eventually became more than £10,000 per calendar month which paid the finance.

However, I felt the builder was getting too comfortable, too greedy and too slow so we needed more of a challenge. Of note the unit at Platt Fold Street was elected for VAT so the pension company could charge me VAT on rents but not vice versa. I mention rough figures here as the rents were being paid directly to the pension company, not the administrators for the commercial lease contracts since November 2019, for over 24 months. Come on, regulated authorities and Mr Legal Ombudsman answer my emails, support small business.

Later during COVID-19, there was a commercial smash and grab of commercial contracts and general business as lenders, pensions and investors went to take funds, contracts and assets. The council, letting agencies, planning and fire regulations, legal protection and insurances were just failing me at every corner. We would eventually start to lose everything in 2020 onwards. The investors now needed me to step up to the plate in 2020/2021. My only available plan of action later was to whistleblow or possibly go to jail for potential contempt of court. What was being exposed were the joint business activities and financial links because of the onerous lending and security demanded by unregulated bridging companies. This is the main theme throughout the book on all UK lending, legals and finances drawing in from what we think - 2015/2016 and culminating in 2020/2021. Then Together Finance crash selling and the brokerage security, just like the Norcross suicide coroner's report, were just allowing all the dominoes to fall down big time. Remember that the Bank of England base rate was at 0.1% APR? Still fighting. Still with me?

'We choose to go to the moon in this decade and do the other things not because they are easy, but because they are hard, because that goal will serve to organise and measure the best of our energies and skills, because that challenge is one that we are willing to accept, one we are unwilling to postpone, and one which we intend to win.'

John F Kennedy

16

100 Lord Street: A Bridge Too Far 2017-2021

I have been told from family and friends (who probably knew only 10% of what was really going on and we come to this point later in the book) that any normal person with my experiences up to now would have simply just walked away to get rid of the sheer damage, unrelenting pressure, humiliation and pain. We shall see the pressures building up to answer that rather blunt statement. I could see all the tell-tale signs building up in the BBC Norcross suicide case article in July 2021 and I could see what he must have been trying to do. Poor fellah. All I now wanted to do was to expose what happened to him and to many other small businesses and embarrass the system into changing and protecting its small businesses, citizens and veterans. It has to. It cannot carry on like this.

I was now just about to set up the exchange on 100 Lord Street. I had the architect lined up from a project before and we were ready to go. To recap, the Cornwall development was sorted, the new build 2-4 Brown Street was finalised, now Platt Fold Street was completed, the terraces were all rented, two build and maintenance businesses were in place, a self-store business was up and running, plus I was coaching and mentoring over two businesses. One of these businesses included setting up 1,000 business accounts with Royal Bank of Scotland for clients who were overseas investors. There is more on this later. 100 Lord Street was now the main project and we were about to press the button. If you think we had problems on what had occurred over the nine years up to now then the next three years would have made any sane normal level headed person hang themselves. We had just experienced a recession, austerity, compliance and regulation. On this project we would now experience probably the weakest political leadership ever in UK politics on the debate over Brexit and miserably ending with the pandemic, albeit with better leadership and opposition. If you weren't thinking of walking away up to this chapter in the business process so far this might possibly tip you over now. Not the Fat Sapper.

In any conflict there is always a silver lining in a sea of despair and funny stories always come out of bad situations. For the decision on 100 Lord Street I needed a clear head and a situation away from the business and family and uniquely this presented itself as a support to a friend wanting to swim the English Channel. About 24 months prior, this friend contacted four mates and said 'get fit, I need support swimmers to swim with me in the channel'. This was Gary 'B', the same chap who got me the airline job. He was now working for Virgin as a Captain and he said I needed to start swimming up to two hours daily with some wild swimming and certainly some rough sea swimming. Using his family and friends' concession ticket with Virgin we went out to Alcatraz to swim to and from the prison in the bay. In the end we could not get a boat pilot in San Francisco so we swam in the bay anyway and got some swimming time in. I also did some sea swimming back in the UK. Then in late September we had a military type week's military 'warning order' to prepare to come to Dover. Forty eight hours later, we all assembled and magically Gary succeeded in swimming the whole crossing in 13.53 hours where us support swimmers all did one hour each. The Channel swimming rules stated that after three hours he could have one other swimmer with him for one hour on and one hour off. My stint was right in the middle of the shipping lanes. It was very bizarre swimming mid-channel with a massive roll on roll off ferry next to our small support fishing boat with Reg the captain. It was just like Captain Pug Wash and the Black Pig complete with an English Channel referee and his support team of mates on board. They were all very good value.

I arrived late and tired having come straight off site so I got my head down for a few hours whilst David, the team captain, had all the drinks and food ready for the big swim which started at something like 3 a.m. Amazingly Gary looked so relaxed he made us all feel as if he would succeed easily. He had done all the work and all the preparation over two years including sleeping cold to condition his body. It is a big commitment. I then got completely stitched up on the big day when they had their cameras and I had to grease Gary all over with insulating fat. The actual 'greasing up' was no worse than being filmed for social media. Stitched up! Great fun team.

Into the English Channel at Dover Gary went and the rest is history. In near perfect conditions combining sea and tide there were several other swimmers and their small support fishing vessels with the latest GPS and echo sounding tech equipment. I think in the end he swam 62 kilometres with the ebb and flood tidal diamond. It was amazing to watch and to experience, especially knowing that his family in France were trying to locate where he was! David, his best mate, did the extra joint swim to help him get him through the last 500-800 metres which with the rip tide is where most fail. (Note to self in business: so near yet so far). The small inflatable then went off to the beach with us moored off. The referee had to see Gary's bare feet on the beach through his binoculars first then the inflatable boat team could recover him. By this stage the team were pretty tired and I, as I had rested, had perked up a bit. When the launch came alongside I could see Gary's body. It seemed very blue and horribly bloated. We got him on board and he was clearly very hypothermic and yours truly then had to get the grease off him before putting his clothing on. I had to do it as the others were tired. I was stitched up again but this time we had to get him warm and quickly. The Commando Arctic Norway training automatically set in.

Joking aside he was very, very cold but he eventually came around wearing a special channel swim outdoor type hooded long coat. We all nursed him back as we returned to Dover. The others relaxed and we kept an eye on him as he drifted in and out of sleep. We recovered and had a beer and Gary's and the team's names were pencilled in on the ceiling of a

Dover pub together with Eddie, his own swim mentor, who had swum the channel previously. This is how this whole channel swim mentoring process works. Next day the guys all bomb burst back to their families and I volunteered to 'shark watch' Gary the whole day while he continued to drift in and out of sleep.

Based on Gary's channel swim preparation, with the confidence, good teamwork and mentors, I then decided I would go ahead and exchange and complete the 100 Lord Street project.

Gary eventually came to and once I thought he was safe medically I headed north. It was a superb result. The things I learned from his experience and his military and aviation background was to have full focus, a detailed plan, a great team like David his team leader, good people like Reg the boat captain and the support swimmers, prepare fully and use your resources for the best success i.e. the tide times, the weather and listen to instructions from the boat's captain. It might seem basic but it worked for me. I wanted his amazing success to rub off on me. Fewer people have swum across the channel than have been to the two Poles and Everest.

We exchanged the next day on 100 Lord Street. Would it be a 'Sea of Despair' or an 'Ocean of Success'? You are about to find out over the next three years, over the fourth phase period of Brexit uncertainty ending, then phase 5, the COVID-19 pandemic. It was the perfect storm in the current sea of seeming tranquility and calm.

As I said before 100 Lord Street was next door to 123 Bradshawgate, the 'Jewel in the Crown' building which had 15 mixed use units of residential and commercial spaces.

100 Lord Street started with 24 units and with help from the Planning Department we ended up with 32 units! This was quite a big increase which I will explain as we go through the chapter. At this time the building had been only really utilising the ground floor with the part assembly of bicycles above and the compressor business only using part of the ground floor. This building was very central in the town but currently only 25% of floor space was used with a large section of at least 10% open to the elements and continually wet through. It was built in 1895 and was in poor condition.

It required a lot of work to protect it from the elements whereas the building next door did not need this level of work. The purchase as we have said was from two parties via their limited companies. One of the parties was, to be honest, a bit greedy in their negotiations because their partner was an ex-lawyer. I seemed to attract them. I wanted to delay the completion which again the lawyer did not want. Sellers would often have no idea what was involved. The Airflow Compressor businessman however, was really good to deal with. He was old school and fully understood the challenges. Also we had completed his works in the previous warehouse that were done to a superb standard even if I say so myself. He was well funded so it all helped being paid on time for this extra work.

The builders were both brothers from the new build project and the previous 15 unit project next door. Paperwork and administration were not their strong point, and like all my projects, I was having to cover all bases which they and their very small skeleton team of labourers saw. Also I was acutely aware of my workload. I was mentoring most weeks so that I could keep up on the bridging costs. The architect and planning was being done but it was incredibly slow and the pressure was beginning to mount up. I had a deep mistrust for the planning system because it was so time consuming and you never knew what you were going to get. The council again also wanted business rates paid from the start date or 'get go' in a building that had had no roof on it for over a year. This again went to a two year tribunal and I refused to pay after the first month. I was now getting totally fed up with the utter greed of local authorities coupled with the total avarice of lenders and lawyers as well as the sheer volume of extra security needed. It was becoming totally ridiculous and it just seemed to be a conflict all the time. There was never any team work and it was never easy, never fun and never fulfilling. Could it ever be? Surely it could *one day?*

The planning was phased in with what was allowed by permitted development i.e. what was allowed without any applications then building up with sequential planning applications. What was interesting was an idea that came from the builders, not the architect. This was a late-stage idea to put another *whole floor* in the building. Remember this was a previous brewery with some storage space underground but this time we elected not to put self-storage *below* but go *up* instead. So what started with 24 units, we then built another floor which added another eight units. This took nearly three years. In hindsight the builder overran by 11 months and the planning and utilities were yet again delayed. I was the cash cow again.

On a positive note, in the whole 100 Lord Street unit, I had roughly assessed twice the number of apartment and shop units next door at a total of 32 as opposed to 15 units in 123 Bradshawgate but this time there was no self-storage and only two car parking spaces. After the English channel swim and making this a 'go' project I wanted 34 rooms in the memory of 33 men and one woman killed on my operations i.e. colleagues who had served our country. Even with all the extra planning we only ended up with 32 shop and apartment units. A bit of military black humour, Chris 'A' got the water metre room and Sarah 'M' got the electricity metre room. Both ironically were killed in one of my old Lynx helicopters with Chris crashing in Bosnia over a minefield and Sarah being hit with a missile in Iraq. They were such great people and so young. Tough times. I got my '34 and more' and am sure they would have been proud in the military black humour way. It might seem a funny or odd way of motivation but it worked for me.

We then did exactly what Ray Croc did at McDonalds in the film 'The Founder' starring Michael Keaton. He marked out, in chalk, on a tennis court the McDonald's kitchen layouts and we did the same on the actual building floors to try and get the extra rooms or beds in. Architects are fine but sometimes on the ground the builder can come up trumps. The key here is that they complement each other which they did eventually.

Some people complained how I approached my projects but like the other 93,000 sq. ft. that I built over 12 years, I always got the projects completed, finished and fully rented. Always. It was just the end exit finance which always caused me issues every single time. Building control as before was OK as we started to build up each apartment and shop. The major issue as always was the speed of the builder, their lack of any paperwork, planning delays and bringing utilities in, especially as the utility company plans of water manifolds and the location of electricity substations were never where they thought they were. We found out later that the builder never even filed accounts at Companies House for a £1,874,000 million build. Odd that.

So what? I was now fully stretched with coaching and mentoring almost every week, the builder seemed to be slow then the bridging finance went to the extension rates of 27% APR (270 times the Bank of England base rate of 0.1% APR). What really did not help was we were now into the full Brexit delay period and were about to end the project into the start of COVID-19. We effectively managed to get the 'S' bridge off the expensive rate and onto Amicus finance. Out of 345 or so lenders, mortgage companies, unregulated lenders and bridging companies the challenger banks were the main clients. If you thought on all our other projects we were having difficulties, this was about to get Herculean. Amicus, the bank, then ran out of money and I had the odds of using a duff lender at 345 to 1. It could only happen to me. And as for the Norcross BBC suicide media case, I was fully beginning to understand the 'system' restrictions while base rates were still at 0.1% APR.

'Try not to become a man of success, but rather become a man of value'.

Albert Einstein

17

Financial Cancer Setting In

The broker that put Amicus together, in my mind, was using templates which were for much bigger projects. JCT 1342 was set up by the architect who was aware of it and I don't think he had used this template before. I was paying for it all through the nose and the architect wanted 50% up front and in my name, not in a company name. Later, when at the end, he sent a bailiff round to recover £500, I understood why. Whilst on the subject we will talk of people not delivering, the architect never even signed the architect's completion certificate on the building so the indemnity insurance cost us more. I assume now I can send a bailiff to him? This was becoming ridiculous in an industry of so called 'professionals' including financiers. Every single time, every single twist and turn, I was getting smashed into. Only this time the finance numbers were double the last project. I kept thinking if any of these guys were on a battlefield they would have been fragged (killed) by their own men. It was mind blowing.

By the second Christmas I was getting late night phone calls from 1 a.m. to 2 a.m. on Friday nights from drunken tradesmen asking to be paid, despite the fact that they always had been paid. They were so drunk they could not even remember calling me. One was a particularly vicious man. At Christmas I put on a basic meal at a simple Toby Carvery and invited 15 tradesmen to say thank you for the year and also to say that I had secured funds for the next three months and that there would be work for January, February and March. I also had provided a modest bottle of wine. Out of the table I had booked for 15, only two turned up. The rest were either out Christmas shopping or on a pub crawl which included the abusive Friday night caller. It seemed I just could not find good people. I started to instigate Saturday workings to get ahead asking one of the brothers to supervise on site which they were paid for. One last item was that we were also getting petty theft on site as the building had three ingress and egress points.

Once, whilst on a rare family break abroad, the builder called me to tell me that someone was walking down the street with my brand new radiators and could *I* lock the door up. I then asked where he was. He told me he was at home as he had left a new joiner in charge on site. I subsequently found out that the full Saturday day rate I was paying for was only from 11:00 a.m. to 2:00 p.m. and not the usual 7:30 a.m. to 4:30 p.m. They could not even get this right. On the subject of family holidays I have never in 12 years since leaving the military ever had an unbroken holiday. I would always have to work 20-25 hours on a week's holiday. I tried to hide it but couldn't do this very well sometimes. The builders would turn their phones off from Friday to Monday and then off again whilst on their holidays. I would always be given the bad news late Friday night every week and invariably as I was boarding my holiday transport. It seemed that I always had bad news to deal with. It was as if I was a voodoo doll with the pins being twisted in even more. I can put up with physical and mental pain and have done so a lot in my life, even by my standards, but this was getting seriously out of hand. I felt this was being done on purpose and I keep a site diary of these sorts of happenings. I always have since the army swimming pool project in the Falklands.

I was making progress with the 100 Lord Street project alongside the coaching and mentoring and I was taking on more and more to make sure I met the payroll commitments every Friday. It was the most horrible pressure to deliver and I felt that the builders, architects and tradesmen were all against me. It was very unpleasant especially as we had two assaults by the main contractor on a joiner and an electrician. Thankfully these events were logged by the police. We later found out that an electrical supplier who thought he was supplying items being paid for by me was making deliveries to another site which one of the contractors was doing on the side. This would come out in the wash later.

I was now at a stage where I had no one to turn to and in my private life I felt the same. I was desperately lonely due to the business pressures. My partner had a very busy career and additionally was extremely occupied with the children and it seemed to be totally unfair to offload my problems onto her. Later she would also get destroyed by lawyers because the Together Finance loans and Whitehall Pensions were lodged in individuals' names and not in limited companies. This was because the financial restrictions were building up and it was the way the banks and brokers had set up the deals - RBS 'enough rope to hang themselves'. The pressure for everyone was just insane. It was just not like this in the military particularly with projects such as the large Falklands swimming pool project. There was just no team. It was all about 'when am I getting paid' every single time. Main suppliers started to pull credit for no reason yet the smaller local Mom and Pop outfits proved better and more flexible than the big boys. I never liked bully boys. The builders, suppliers, lawyers and banks were all the same. It seemed the bigger the outfit the worse they were.

I really enjoyed the mentoring and coaching despite the workload. I knew I was gaining huge experience and although a quiet person I enjoyed working with clients and would also teach larger groups of up to 150 people in seminars around the world for a third party $100 million training organisation. In fact I taught over 2,000 students on these seminars worldwide. I think I was pretty good (high average again) and I was awarded the International Mentor of the Year Award covering 25 countries so I must have been doing something right. I was mentoring, doing weekend courses and meeting my payroll commitments. I was relatively comfortable as I had done my numbers and knew we would have a 32 unit mixed use incoming generating asset with all my same team involving builders, architect, surveyors, planners, building control and lettings manager, a stereotype of the same project next door, same town, same everything despite all the previous problems. I had de-risked it all but the entry and exit finance was the bit that would bring more and more risk. This was due to the compliance and regulation and the financiers and lawyers making more complications, more delays and yet more costs.

The mentoring at one stage did get a bit like the military and airlines on duty, i.e. 'H' can you cover all this extra work?' They would ask if I would help out as others could not... I just got on with it. Over a three week period I was booked to do three London mentorships from Tuesday to Thursday each week then go home every other week or on site. Over that three week period I instead went to Hong Kong and Singapore over the two weekends to help cover. I would jump on a Heathrow jet on Thursday night overnight business class to each location. I would then cover Friday, Saturday and Sunday and then return overnight on Sunday. I would sleep all the way back and do my laundry on Monday ready to start mentoring again on Tuesday. After three weeks of mentoring and a Hong Kong and Singapore weekend I poured myself into bed at home. I then slept for 24 hours, not unlike in the military.

The groups abroad were good although the pressure to sell was intense. I did learn a lot about sales and I enjoyed airline flying as I knew exactly what was going on behind the scenes and I always tried to be nice to the cabin crew who work very hard. I flew Business Class for the third party organisation but for my own business abroad I always flew Premium Economy to keep my costs down. This meant you could work and have slightly better lounges so it was a balance of cost and a good work environment. I approached the third party organisation and asked why they did not do the cheaper air travel and split the difference but I was ignored. Bigger pockets I guess.

I mostly felt like I lived in two worlds. I had a real world existence and a sort of Alice in Wonderland existence with the training and travel and then the other world of the building site. I hope and I think I did deliver on the mentoring, coaching and the course presentations which I worked hard at with a nice lady called Harriet. You would get scored and the organisation would take it seriously. The adage, you can please some of the people all of the time or all of the people some of the time was all so true. The course attendees could be pretty blunt with their comments and amateurs could be pretty scathing on their feedback. This was dimly viewed by the organisation. It took a lot of work to do this plus other business commitments. Business can be harsh like the battlefield. Get on with it 'H'.

Someone might be shy or maybe not a natural presenter but if you know your stuff and are passionate in my mind you cannot fake it. I see property and business trainers all the time and if anyone is six months out of date or off tune it stands out a mile and the audience will spot a fake a mile away. I always like to be real and even with failure I like to be honest with people. People who fail make the best trainers in the world. If they have had real palpable pain and are natural givers they will share and want to help others not to make the same mistakes. Greedy takers in life can go to hell in my mind, I have always hated greedy selfish people. In the military people who have struggled often make good leaders and specialist instructors and are 'often people's people' because of this. For me, ice cold natural pilots don't make good instructors. Post COVID-19 I forecast a change where the pressure for success might be better served by people who have really struggled and who can be closer to the audience. This is now much more real world and I see coaching and mentoring going this way. We have a duty in the industry and in life to do this.

I have attended conferences where you become motivated by speakers such as Richard Branson, Alan Sugar, Tony Robbins, Tim Peake, Ranulph Fiennes and others. Sometimes I would attend but I would often go and speak to a secondary lower-level speaker who is in the subject area and who I really liked because I wanted a certain piece of information or a book signed. This, like property training and business coaching, e.g. Rich Dad or Success Resources is a huge industry. For me I think it boils down to chemistry and whether you like that person's personality and you could work together. Shouty meet shouty, mouse meet mouse, or maybe chalk and cheese. I think it is very personal for coaching and mentoring.

I started to put together my own training weekends near Wigan which I did for my experience profile and for the fact that I could show people around my live real projects. I think over two or three years this really helped my profile and bring people on well in their training. Like the military I never liked theory, I was always in the real world, sometimes maybe too much.

100 Lord Street continued unabated. We had the ground and second floor pretty much sorted so we then set about constructing the extra floor. In hindsight the roof and extra floor should have been done first. The architect was not the lead here oddly and I think although the builder was actively delaying the site progress, the fundamental idea was sound. I

will do the numbers shortly but the extra floor would add value to the building of an extra 33%, potentially nearly £700,000 GDV. I just had to balance the cost benefit analysis.

At the time of writing and once 100 Lord Street was signed off for 32 (34) 'room' units, I had at this stage developed 93,000 sq. ft. in 12 years of building space covering Portsmouth, Bristol, Cornwall, Wigan and Greater Manchester. If you take the normal market GDV the total developed valuation came to £7,850,000 and the gross rents totalled £522,000. That was for a small series of companies and 200 rental units, including self-storage and car park spaces. I was really proud of this. I now had a good measure of developing terraces, apartments, retail shops, pod offices, car park areas, self-storage, lease options and new builds. I mentored and coached over 2,000 people in the UK and abroad with both military and civilian clients and we maintained properties and additionally had a rental business, so I felt the profile was good. My ongoing unease understandably was with the demands from my investors together with the continually increasing bridging costs and the exit finance which always seemed so 'non concrete' to use a building term. These never ever filled me with confidence and this was getting worse over time.

So what? On the 100 Lord Street numbers I effectively put in about £1,874,000 on a three storey unit I thought would GDV at £1,900,000 to £2,000,000 with a gross rent roll of £172,500. This would gross yield at 9% so with a 75% LTV on the commercial exit loan we would fit in as many units as we could. I was acutely aware of the time and finance costs which were mounting up with delays. My investors, once the bridging was released, would average 9.2% APR over the period. So with the mentoring income and with the expectation that the longer term military guys at that percentage investor return rate, 50% of the team would be onboard for a protracted term. So maybe this was not a bad summary of expectation overall.

I was now again very nervous about the RICS surveys and over 123 Bradshawgate and 100 Lord Street I must have spent over £15,000 on six surveys to try and get the best and most sensible RICS business valuations. A proper survey valuation company called Sanderson Weatherall with Nick Heap worked best for us. The full market appraisal for 123 Bradshawgate and 100 Lord Street were respectively £925,000 and £1,900,000. Both of these were figures I could work with and Nick was very fair. The key was whether they appeared on the exit lender's chosen panel. This I started to find totally unworkable. Lenders would, it seemed, have one survey valuer with an instruction to down value. It was a simple collaboration and every time you felt as if you had worked 100 hour weeks, missed holidays and anniversaries only for them to down value. In all honesty I found it all to be rather depressing. A stark example was you may recall St Eval in Cornwall where we end valued at £150,000 and had only five out of eight mortgages so then we had to find a mortgage host. Today they value at £250,000 each so those eight units would now be worth £2 million. Why is this continued RICS survey nonsense? I felt as if the Royal 'Warrant' should be removed.

Coaching and Mentoring groups.

Eclectic tenants - churches to kid's gyms.

To hairdresser tenants.

*To vegan coffee
shop tenants.*

*Cars and bikes
to raise finance.*

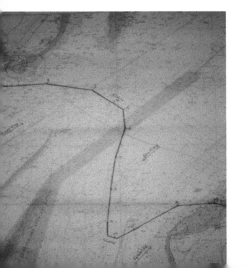

*Gary's successful Channel
swim 62 km. I swam
an hour with him in
the middle. His success
inspired 100 Lord Street.*

Gary's successful English Channel swim. Do anything you want to – in 13.53 hrs. BZ to him and the other support swimmers.

Astronaut Tim Peake's advice to me. A great Ambassador for the AAC.

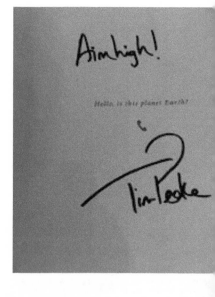

My vision board all things in the past. I also had one of the family next to it. Anything to keep going vs the banks.

Platt Fold Street ex four x five-year leases. Ongoing with Legal Ombudsman. £100,000 plus per annum in rents.

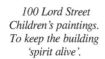

100 Lord Street Children's paintings. To keep the building 'spirit alive'.

Covid 19 Busters 11,988 sets of PPE. To try to keep the banks onboard.

Rt Hon Andy Burnham MP and Leigh. Mayor opening 123 Bradshawgate. Restricted lending on the shops 2015.

123 Bradshawgate built in 1876. Photo taken circa 1898 with horses and gas lamps in colour. Beautiful.

123 Bradshawgate before

123 Bradshawgate after – any lending? RICS surveys varied from £225k, £295k, £495k, £855k, £925k. Totally unbelievable. Together Finance and Duff & Phelps crash sale 2020.

Outright winner of seven UK property awards.

TV star Mike Norcross suicide BBC coroner's report – my sincerest thoughts to his family. I know what he was going through. Ridiculous security and poor expensive lending. RIP Sir.

Bank of England Governor and the RBS scandal article – courtesy BBC business lending restricted.

You can't build, build, build if you don't have the money

Paul Keddy laments cautious lending that keeps the UK short of new homes

Bailey for clo at len small

Superb quality of UK media on lending practises of UK finance leading up to with COVID-19 from Andrew Verity at BBC, Paul Keddy at the 'i' newspaper and James Hurley at the Times – restricted lending again.

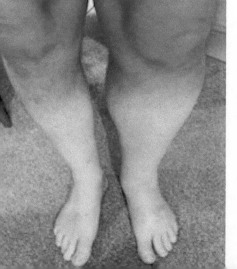

DVT Wigan Court Whitehall 23rd March and 4th May. The leg was twice the size three hours before. The lawyers knew this yet put me into administration that hour. Is this how we bully and treat individuals and small business owners?

*12 years - 10
ltd companies
and Hatchard
Homes Limited.*

*Book publishing to
raise more money.*

*100 Lord Street
next to 123
Bradshawgate.
Both International
Award nominees
£82,000 and
£170,000 per annum
rents. Lending?*

Coaching and mentoring more finance raised to try and keep the bank onside.

Fat Sapper hence the book name! One of 11 companies to keep the buildings rents alive 30,900 plus meals.

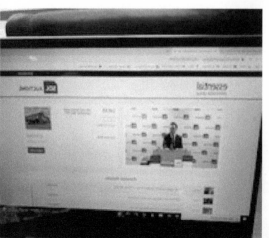

100 Lord Street - crash sale reserve £1,050,000 a 'loss' of £850,000! SDL Auctioneer quote 'bargain of century' vs Together Finance and Duff & Phelps. Online auction filmed and recorded.

Drying clothes in the car - no money. My second-hand – 'Sea King helicopter' from the Iraq days. I lived in this car on odd days during COVID-19. £50,000 pcm to £1,351 pcm after 23rd March 2020 after crash house sales.

Car hire care sales anything to raise finance. I even did Audi gear boxes!

100 Lord Street and 123 Bradshawgate. On crash bank sale there was a Land Registry title dispute over one parking space!

*COVID-19 emergency NHS housing we tried
everything to stop banks crash selling our units.
10 units £800,000 of pressure crash sales.*

*100 Lord Street - in the memory of 34 killed soldiers. The banks
were just never interested in lending 2015-2020. £1,900,000
RICS reserve set £1,050,000. The culmination of 12 years
of work all for absolutely nothing. £6 million of property
and £1.5 million of limited companies all potentially lost.*

*'When something is important enough, you
do it even if the odds are not in your favour.
Some people don't like change, but you need to
embrace change if the alternative is disaster.
if you get up in the morning and think the
future is going to be better, it is a bright day'.*

Elon Musk

18

Dark Clouds

Dark clouds. I mention this here and this should be a pivot for the book. The foundation stone of my 12 years in business was developing properties but the cancer of finance was setting in as restrictions and security were becoming increasingly so large and onerous. This is I believe from the Coroner's report, why Mike Norcross the TV star and developer sadly committed suicide as shown in the BBC July 2021 published report. Also one of my third party suppliers was found dead and I was to be put under the Secretary of Business 'Suicide Watch'. Dark clouds indeed.

I also want to go into detail on why, in about September 2019, I went into a form of personal lock down on the developing site and why I was in that state for six months before COVID-19. The simple reason was that I had financed the 100 Lord Street unit with 'S' bridging, then Amicus, then back to 'S' bridging, where over a year their extension fees went up to 27% APR. We were nearing completion and I needed to get another lender, remembering that exit lending 2015-2019 was starting to become more and more difficult. Paraphrasing the three brokers who worked on loans with 'S', 'C' and 'E' and 'W' with Together Finance they all seemed to come up with my Asset and Liability sheet of approximately the same at £9,047,000. This included £6 million of property which admittedly had £2 million of life assurance, a lease option of approximately £1,675,000 GDV, 11 limited companies with evaluations pre-COVID-19 of £1.5 million, a rent roll of £400,000 plus and two salaries. In short this was a herculean amount of assets just as in the Mike Norcross case. To put this in context another investor working on his own projects had just had an offer of a £1.5 million loan at 3% APR which is exactly what I was after in May 2018. Why not me after 12 years of *my* hard work? The broker said it was my profile, my credit rating, then it was the post code, then the covenant (strength) of the tenant, then the sun, the rain, the snow, then the football, the rugby and so it continued. It seemed they looked for any excuse not to lend to me and I was getting beaten down every time. There was no proper commercial exit mortgage lending ever and the loan to value assessments were getting worse and worse. Lenders were simply not interested in property and they were certainly not interested in mixed use or commercial property. Brokers and property investing training companies seemed to be becoming oblivious to this. I did not want this industry to be about the middle men making all the profits whilst the real risk taking people in the 'arena' were getting nothing at all and were being damaged when loans were pulled under duress.

In essence my loan was now £300,000 short as Together Finance now would only offer £1.2 million at 12% APR with a 16% to 17% extension stringer rate. So we had the secondary bridge at 27% APR. For balance, before the bank and pension came wading in, the 'S' loan was actually one northern investor who not only tried to help get a buyer for 100 Lord Street but offered his loan at capital only. This was Steve 'F' who had lost nearly everything back in 2008 and 2009 as had so many others with the banks' actions. In a word – he had integrity. This was set up with pension funds renegotiated to sit outside of the Land Registry as were my unsecured investors. The building had the commercial units completed and were about 75% filled, the apartments were 90% complete but were all empty. I was assured yet again by the broker we could get a further top up loan later in the year once they were finished and filled. One of the builder brothers, the bully boy Thomas 'G' locked the site down before Christmas, stole the keys and was feeding his own project with my supplies and to add insult to injury he was not insured for the Party Wall Act claim against his new build. He then demanded an extra £75,000 bonus to release the keys demanding a forced signature which my lettings manager was not allowed to witness and who was, quote, 'bullied' out of the meeting. This was witnessed as such with evidence on my phone. I signed under duress just to get control of the site back and get *my* keys back for *my* building and not void the insurance. In Donald Trump's 'The Art of the Deal' he talks of his father's rough construction background. Many investors now understand this industry.

Then, in about two more months on site, the other OK builder Peter 'G' finished off and building control (not the architect) signed it off. Over the next five months I filled all the retail units and about 75% of the apartments. Later, post March 2020, the bully builder then, to add insult to injury, leafleted the whole high street with a photo of me comparing me to the virus namely COVID-19.

I informed the police explaining the circumstances and citing defamation and I received a logged report number. It took me a day to clean off all the glued leaflets on the 100 shops and ATMs. I had to repaint the whole of 123 Bradshawgate and 100 Lord Street due to the mess which cost £1,100. Still reading, still with me? This was all filmed and recorded. With terrorists at least you know the enemy and what they will do within reason. These so-called professionals just kept coming at me again and again. Financiers and lawyers would be later. Keep going 'H'.

On my side of the JCT build contract for 100 Lord Street, the wages were being paid but the building had not yet been signed off by the architect. Also the builders did not sign off the JCT 1342 contract and the 12 months of snagging was never covered which cost me an extra £1,667. Stores with a value estimated at £20,000 were taken off site and stolen according to the main electrical supplier and one tradesman. And then the Party Wall Act claim went to litigation over £36,000 with Jazz Hairdressing and the cost of the site closure on bridging cost me about £21,000. That Falklands swimming pool project looked to be on planet Mars and was now a long and distant pleasant memory. This builder damage alone cost over £77,000 of extra fees. I would have been happy to pay a sensible bonus to the OK builder's brother subject to refinance, although the refinance never came about with COVID-19. To close this rather nasty chapter the bully builder burst into my office in October 2020 and threatened to 'smack my face in'. My reply was that I had filmed it all to which his lawyer's reply was that I never asked permission and it was thus inadmissible in court. He was one of life's bullies for sure. Then the real financial issues started in earnest. Business is a jungle out there so be prepared.

With the investors, because of the lending restrictions, I had put the Business Loan Agreements in Hatchard Homes Limited and my website name. I had an audit trail with my payments into a private account named 'JPH' and into Hatchard Developments Limited. I thought this was simple and straightforward involving my Natwest bank accounts. We used templated Business Loan Agreements from a solicitor's practice exactly as many SMEs did to keep costs down and as a lettings agency had also used templates for the commercial leases on 100 Lord Street and 123 Bradshawgate, no problems there. We had other businesses that used this exact same template procedure during COVID-19 for their grants and who subsequently received money from Wigan Council but I was turned down using the exact same legal type template. I carried out my own internal investigation of the Hatchard group and realised that I had approximately eight plus small loans, one of which was a large extension loan anyway. In hindsight I should have put 'pax persona' and signed the signatures on behalf of the other partner. However, we still had a full audit trail as to where funds were lodged for the development and on audit with Natwest Online and my accountant Norton Tax.

Of note, the investor's lawyer who I had spoken to had email evidence from me that we were still waiting for proper exit lending. That lawyer I believe was receiving £5,000 per client which was simply fees for the misery of finance being pulled. Luke Johnson was being proved so right. I have been very measured with my language throughout the book but I could swear to high heaven right now. You can now sense my growing anger in the latter stages of the book. How many small businesses and individuals have had to suffer this?

I now had the 100 Lord Street building finished. I was wanting the same RICS surveyor to carry out the further survey and obviously add value to the building and get what is technically called a loan extension and not a further advance. This meant that I could at least pay off some of the expensive lending and some interest from my investors. For some reason Together Finance kept delaying the survey instruction from September 2018 until about February 2019, funny that. By which time the investors' lawyers never served papers or witnessed the action but put Hatchard Homes Limited straight into administration. This I only learned about after coming back from a short family break at my accountants.

Since the property was in private names and not a limited company, it was 'fraud' apparently, stated by a lawyer whom I talked at length with mid summer over the process and emailed (recorded). It was the bridging company who declared they would not lend in a company structure, and hence the reason why the private names were given for the lending. Funny, I was sure at the time that the Land Registry clearly showed all the properties in the two individual names (as all our investment properties always have been), and also the Sanderson Weatherall RICS survey reports sent to all investors were in the same two names. There was always a full and open source of information supplied continually over 24 months with the surveys dated 9th August and 17th August 2018 for 100 Lord Street and 123 Bradshawgate which I constantly emailed and drew attention to *all* investors. That legal firm and the not serving and not witnessing issue is currently being investigated by the Legal Ombudsman. One thing COVID-19 has produced is a band of keyboard warriors who know everything. Fifty one investors have the original 24 emails over 24 months with this very clearly shown. So we now have 51 'witnesses' plus all the support businesses. People can litigate and damage or their legal teams can *actually read* the emails and evidence. Keep fighting, keep informing and updating everyone 'H' since COVID-19 was looming...

Just so I do not lose you, the Legal Ombudsman at the time of writing is investigating the extra top up loan requested from Gunson, the RICS surveyor acting for Together Finance. Remember that it was delayed by the lender who then took extra bridging fees over for another six months. And note that the building on the first Gunson survey was unfinished and had at that time seven out of 32 units filled. This was now completely finished, the full building control was signed off and it was insured for £2.3 million with a rebuild quote of £3.6 million! It now also had an occupancy of 25/32 units. The Gunson RICS surveyor kept the same value and now this meant no more lending!

This was utterly beyond comprehension and unbelievable.

And the UK public are incredulous as to why the high street and commercial premises are dying yet with all the huge 'finance carrying' costs and increasingly onerous security homes and pensions just as in the Norcross BBC investigation case and in my mind 'fraudulent' RICS valuation surveys this was becoming clear to me. Businesses cannot carry on like this when the Bank of England base rates are 0.1% APR. The week the Together Finance loan was eventually assembled in May 2018, I had the Whitehall pensions then arranged and sitting underneath the first charge on the property plus over 1,500 miles I drove that very week to try to coordinate it all. My legal team drove from Essex to Longleat to help oversee the paperwork. This was more than a herculean workrate to try and make it all work. Both organisations were then to pull out later in COVID-19.

We subsequently found out that Gunson had had their professional indemnity insurance premium increased by 400% because another developer had claimed similar survey undervaluations on previous works which now affected my loan increase. And I was being accused of fraud! Just to complete the exit lending fiasco here and to mirror Cornwall 300 miles away and this unregulated lender practice of extension fees, COVID-19 then set in and immediately Together Finance would not allow forbearance. This was despite the fact that in March 2020 we had 98.2% occupancy, admittedly with a few tenants on payment plans. Additionally Wigan Council were delaying our supposed mandatory grants on our units which then came to nothing. They were simply blocking us with evidence from other SMEs locally. The local MP is investigating this now.

I find it incomprehensible that, for example, the FCA's Chief Executive Officer who is on a £455,000 per annum salary cannot investigate my case. Most other Government regulatory authority CEOs are all on salaries of £180,000 plus and offer the same, i.e. no service. I just wanted people to do their jobs and take mine and others' cases on.

So what? Other mitigating circumstances were that the

bridging loans being set up by brokers charged us £15,000-£20,000 for the product, plus we had so much security that we had to provide in our own names, not in a limited company as previously stated. This included my PPR (Personal Primary Residence) i.e. my own home as security. The later regulated investigation by the Financial Ombudsman would now be stipulated as a regulated, not unregulated loan investigation quote Royal Bank of Scotland 'enough rope to hang themselves' because I had to use the main home as extra security. The building in question was worth £1,900,000, the building next door worth £925,000 and had over £400,000 of gross rents, including lease sublet rents on a warehouse with a GDV of £1,765,000, plus we had a small amount of shares and our salaries. Some investors' lawyers took this as fraud concerning the own names part. Again the brokers were creating a fall guy with no limited company protection as we were now exposed and the very few aggressive investors' lawyers were smashing through on this technicality. Additional personal guarantees required in the property investing industry then take away any limited company protection anyway hence the increasing litigation and the rise in insurance for Personal Indemnity. I could now see exactly what had occurred with Mike Norcross in just the same way and this is the key to the whole raison d'etre of the book. This is absolutely true and unbelievable and why so many businesses were starting to be smashed into by the banks, the lawyers and the courts.

'Genius is one percent inspiration and ninety-nine percent perspiration'

'I have not failed. I've just found 10,000 ways that don't work'.

'Our greatest weakness lies in giving up. The most certain way to succeed is always to try just one more time'.

Thomas Edison

19

Pulling the Funding: Unregulated Bridging Company

Together Finance and their lawyers Duff & Phelps *immediately* pulled the loan two months into COVID-19 despite me asking for forbearance with the Wigan Council grant applications (recorded). A few details to add to the flames of despair, the main family home, 123 Bradshawgate and 100 Lord Street were all used by Together Finance as onerous and extra security (total value £3.25 million just as in the Norcross BBC case) and were immediately crash sold via online auctions within four months of the COVID-19 protocols starting officially on 23rd March 2020. At that time 23 eligible business grants with Wigan Council and the Government never happened. These had a collective value of £130,000 over 11 limited companies in 2020-2021, a value which just did not materialise.

Later we asked the Financial Ombudsman to seek

compensation of over £350,000 which was not awarded as they have stated that this is an unregulated case and still do now despite the family home having been used as security and is now 'lost'. Other lawyers' groups state that the main home security makes it a regulated investigation and therefore allowable for compensation. This is now being re-investigated yet again with MP support and the petition, the media and the book process. The UK media at the time of writing in Autumn 2021, are constantly reporting on the FCA, the Fraud Office, the Financial Ombudsman, Citizens Advice and Trading Standards service which are being reported as below quality from comments from UK citizens. The Financial Ombudsman reports in the Daily Mail that there are up to three years of delays to deal with cases! The forced property sales in 2020-2021 lost us on the market about £1.1 million plus the damaged lease on Platt Fold Street lost us a further £600,000 of potential equity. The family home was then bought out by a limited company who took ownership after bullying pressure by the administrators for Together Finance. (This was recorded on the phone also by third parties). Then the Together Finance onerous 'triple property £3,250,000 value security' (main home, 123 Bradshawgate and 100 Lord Street), when the main home was crash sold, that security then passed back to the 123 Bradshawgate building, which when that was crash sold, the security was passed back finally onto the actual development project of the 100 Lord Street building. Still with me?

A nice Iraqi gentleman bought 123 Bradshawgate with a limited company for £800,000 (GDV £925,000 on a RICS survey so losing £125,000 of value). Note the Bank of

England base throughout was 0.1% APR and we now had two bridging loans sitting at 17% and 27% APR (Steve 'F' from the previous note was trying to help). So finance borrowing rates increased during COVID-19 some 170-270 times the base rate! Technically the Iraqi gentleman could have gone to the forced Together Finance, Duff & Phelps and SDL Property Auction online and potentially bought it at a much lower crash sale price but he stuck to his offer which I thought was very fair and just. Some have intimated that somehow my six Iraq tours were involved in the convenient sale of 123 Bradshawgate to an Iraqi citizen. It is amazing what is said and misunderstood in times of financial stress and pressure circumstances. At the time we offered 100 Lord Street to him as well because of the Together Finance and their agent Duff & Phelps crash selling process. His agent said at the time it was a 'superb building, well maintained and managed'. They were from London and had a huge portfolio around the UK or so I was informed.

Together Finance then forced an immediate online auction sale on 100 Lord Street on 31st July 2021 with SDL Property Auctions. There was falsification of the Gross Development Value, the actual rents and a Land Registry dispute on the building next door due to *one* car parking space. There was manipulation of the original RICS valuation and continued restricted loans based on the Gunson valuation. Additionally two buyers were wilfully blocked from buying pre-auction, one with an actual live commercial mortgage offer (with evidence from Aldermore bank). Lastly there was one big investor who was really kindly and genuinely trying to help. The auction on 31st July was pulled by the SDL Property

Auction chief auctioneer, Andrew Parker. As it was online it was all via mobile phones and texts used as the only way to try to stop the crash selling. To cut a long and very painful story short, 100 Lord Street was eventually 'crash sold' by Together Finance on the next SDL Property Auction on 30th September 2020 with Duff & Phelps misrepresenting the rents and GDV again. The third party involved who was aware of this is now dead. I had investors on the phone crying on both auction dates. Forbearance on commercial loans in the UK during COVID-19 was publicly in the media space. I am now, for the record, telling the nation it was complete and utter nonsense. I still have the recording of the auction. David smashed into by Goliath. Let us get back up and fight.

Remember the Sanderson Weatherall valuation I told you about on 100 Lord Street? The Duff & Phelps reserve this time was set at £1,050,000 which would have lost another £850,000. Duff & Phelps legals made £50,000 from the crash sale. I was furious with the greedy banks and the even greedier lawyers destroying my family, my properties and soon all my limited companies. We have since found out that these two companies have a horrendous reputation in this industry regardless of COVID-19. The buyer with the mortgage in his hand had to go to auction and he actually purchased the property for £1,270,000 which was some £630,000 less than the market GDV, his company was called '34ANDMORE Limited'. Funny name that. I was sure we had 34 killed soldiers in their memory in the building. I have subsequently found out that the purchaser used the same bank Aldermore I had used seven years previously on the building next door, 123 Bradshawgate. They still, in 2021, have no lending on the retail space. Totally unbelievable yet again and here I am today fighting for my financial life to expose this industry. It does not have to be like this after all the hard work of normal average citizens, business owners and in many cases, veterans. People are being treated like idiots. I will go through the total damage of the whole Hatchard group caused by this action later as we build the circumstances around the unregulated bridging industry and what banks, lawyers and courts have really done to people and business in COVID-19. Two charities were then taken out of our business because of this. I was gutted over the damage to the charities. With marathons and triathlons over 30 years I had raised a very modest and quiet £12,000 plus donations, as many average citizens do every day and I was hardly a Captain Tom! I now had two charities in buildings which we lost plus I had been advising a charity for homeless ex-servicemen in Wiltshire. It was ok though as the bank made an extra £100,000 on the Lord Street loan now crash selling and the lawyer made £50,000. A normal person would just swear here, keep fighting 'H'.

So what? If you are still standing, well done. That was a lot for anyone reading to take on board. A businessman having to contend with this over three years and to keep going with 51 investors and 32 plus creditors now sitting outside and a pension plan crashing into the 11 limited companies and HMRC chasing too, how would he keep going? It was just too unbelievable.

I had to take stock and clearly it was pretty obvious by now the family had to cut away from me which culminated with a divorce in late 2020. This was if nothing else for all of our safety and protection. I was both heartbroken and devastated. Fifteen years of marriage, 12 years in business, all the £6 million of property and 11 companies valued at £1.5 million, with accusations of fraud, lodged assault and abuse were all yet to come. If I did not have the bit between my teeth to take on the banks, courts and lawyers I did now... My father always taught me to fight. This was now the fight of my life and I was going to win.

'One of the ways to get out of a tight box is to invent your way out'

Jeff Bezos

20

Smash and Grab

Divorce. This was really sad as between us we had served in the military for 42 years. It had to come to this due to the lenders and lawyers and soon to be the courts' actions simply pulling the loans. Remember that overall in 12 years my Hatchard group had developed £7,850,000 GDV and had a rent roll of £522,000 and had 11 limited companies that were either breaking even or creating a small profit. In twelve years I didn't take anything for myself from the business ever. However, there was just no exit lending. We built up effectively from 2015/2016 to 2019 and then were exposed by the damage trigger, COVID-19. Then a pension company, Whitehall and HMRC filed against me personally twice both on 23rd March and 4th May 2021 whilst I was undergoing serious DVT treatment (witnessed by the family doctor. The documentation, emails and calls are all proof. See photos). This triggered the loss of the 11 limited company directorships. Now with the TM01 action, the process of handing over the directorships to UK Companies House resulted in my now being put under an industry 'suicide watch' with Dorset and Wigan Police and my family doctor.

I had now started to be threatened by contempt of court as a single now unrepresented citizen faced with a potential prison sentence. I felt disgusting, dirty, just a common criminal and also that I was the black sheep of the family. A family member confided that he cried at night because of the arguments. I was totally humiliated and felt that I was now perceived to be a complete failure. I was throwing up most mornings. I think this was due to the DVT medications and was trying to get exercise of sorts, to get out and see the sun and breathe some fresh air. Anything to keep going, like most family separations because of COVID-19, the whatsapp films, pictures of the kids, the pets, and them on small holiday breaks all really helped. This kept me positive and moving on despite the damaging actions of the lawyers and at times bullying of the lawyers themselves. Nothing was going to stop me.

Wigan Court was presented with my unregulated lending files and spreadsheets yet the second time I was in hospital they did not open any files and were too busy to stop the personal administration against me. They knew I was hospitalised twice in March and May 2021 suffering a serious illness. This is recorded on the phone and there is evidence from the doctor as detailed above. I was then told by the Clerk of the Court for the Wigan judge on the phone the following Monday 'he is busy and is two months behind schedule, you will have to sort it out now with the lawyers' (recorded).

One of my long-term third party team members in

another business walked out after 12 years after supporting me by overseeing the Duff & Phelps action. He was also overseeing the lawyer field team acting for the Secretary of State for business and Durkan trustees in May to June 2021 and was part of the meeting with the bullying of that particular builder in October 2020. He sadly died later that year after I personally supported him.

I was then told the divorce was 'convenient'. This came from the Secretary of State for Business on site visit lawyer (this is recorded). I was now in utter complete disbelief. Sixteen months of COVID-19 and now this. Everything to absolutely nothing. It felt like 'warrior to criminal' overnight going back to 18 years ago when the police gave me that driving ticket in Bristol. My mother then quoted my father, after he had helped shoot the herd during the BSE crisis on the farm all those years back, "H' you have got to get up and fight back in your father's memory'. My mother was probably deep down a bigger fighter than my father.

Wigan Court was presented with my unregulated lending files and spreadsheets yet the second time I was in hospital they did not open any files and were too busy to stop the personal administration against me. They knew I was hospitalised twice in March and May 2021 suffering a serious illness. This is recorded on the phone and there is evidence from the doctor. I was then told by the Clerk of the Court for the Wigan judge on the phone the following Monday - 'he is busy and is two months behind schedule you will have to sort it out now with the lawyers' (recorded).

I have six emails from one of the unregulated lenders stating 'let's bully and harass him' against me on file. The main bridging loan was effectively from one wealthy man in London who was the source of the bullying on file and the emails from him direct to that lending company. At Sandhurst we all respected the two Army Captains, Nairac and Westmacott, whose paintings were hanging in pride of place and we all wanted to be them in conduct if not bravery. I was supposed to be wanting to build up business and wealth ethically for my investors first then family second. If this is what money did to so-called successful people I was now just not interested at all. Greed and bullying, why not be ethical and have sensible margins for everyone? This can all work, just don't be greedy. 1,500% APR payday loans and 27% APR build loans are just not sustainable. COVID-19 kills so do lenders, pensions, lawyers, courts and brokers. The film starring Daniel Craig in the Layer Cake was absolutely spot on, showing the pecking order of private lenders and the sinister, dark and threatening side to the industry. As before one bridging investor Steve 'F' however was more lenient in balancing this restricted industry. He was fair and I am personally a very fair man. Something had to give.

The other property partner was now effectively being blackmailed and was even threatened with administration from a mortgage lender with a charity in one of the terrace buildings. The Government had put an eviction moratorium on owners and landlords who had been disallowed access to try to sell on the market. In July 2020 this eviction moratorium by the Government went to nine months on commercial tenants so owners and landlords potentially had to put up with either partial or no rents by law and have access blocked by tenants. Lenders just pulled the finance with no forbearance whatsoever.

All this was now very serious and totally damaging. Why was the Legal Ombudsman taking over 13 weeks to answer an email? Long lost friends and family were wondering where I was and what was going on and why am I so busy? Why the separation? Why the failing health? Why the suicide watch? Reading this you *all* know now. 'H' just keep trying, keep moving, don't be a target. It is the same on the battlefield or in business.

I was really proud of my service to my country in my military career hence the lengthy outline at the start. This is so you get some measure of me and all is recorded on file as you would expect. In business, we had a total GDV of £7,850,000 and had total gross rents of £522,000 built up in 12 years. Likewise up to COVID-19 I was very proud of the property and small business industry which included 200 rental units, 144 tenants kept going through COVID-19, 12,000 sets of PPE sold, 2,000 students coached and mentored, 2,700 cars disinfected, 20 sets of NHS emergency accommodation offered through COVID-19, 30,900 hot meals cooked by the take out Fat Sapper, five UK landlord awards, two UK small developer awards, two International Development nominations (ironically on 123 Bradshawgate and 100 Lord Street), an International Mentor award covering 25 countries worldwide, 51 investors serviced up until COVID-19, 144 units cleaned and maintained, 1,000 overseas bank accounts set up for overseas investors, two published books, £6 million of GDV sales including the lease option, £1,485,000 of business rates and council tax paid into Wigan borough on 200 refurbished units and 11 limited companies from medium operations to start ups. Subject to the Legal and Finance Ombudsman and Trustee investigations now potentially all are lost. No, I must fight now. Something had to get out into the media otherwise we will have a generation of business leaders and entrepreneurs who will lay down their weapons and just not bother.

I am an average man just doing an average job having spent 18 years in the military, two years in airline flying and 12 years working in property. Today nothing is left with all the above potentially completely lost subject to the Secretary of State trustee and now the Legal Ombudsman intervention leaving me nothing but my £44 a day pension. A petition was raised at Parliament to expose the industry. This was not for me but for my investors and teams. You and my investors might like to ask me why? Keep fighting as my father told me.

So what? This book has been written to right a monumental wrong and get my name back, my companies back and get my integrity and respect renewed with family, friends and my various military and civilian families. It is not about the money for me. Personally it is about sorting right from wrong and if successful you can be the judge as the book sales will simply pay my investors back and show the world there has to be another way financially.

I read a book once about a soldier who was captured and interrogated in Iraq and said afterwards if he met his interrogator and captor today he would 'slot' him. If I met the banks, courts and the lawyers that did this to me and my family and associates above I would also 'slot' them all. You can all define the word 'slot'. Mike Norcross, rest in peace, my friend.

'It pays to know the enemy – not least because at some time you may have the opportunity to turn him into a friend'

Margaret Thatcher

21

Mindset, Protect, Recover, Adapt, Overcome and Win

I think by all accounts anyone reading up to this stage would by anyone's measure realise that this was a pretty dire position to be in. Personally I was beyond anger and desperation and the low points were many and way more especially since September 2019 when I went into my own personal lockdown. Someone close to me and some quiet people in the background, great friends who had all probably identified six occasions where they just could not get hold of me, were really worried. I will come back to this aspect and why six months before COVID-19 I was becoming incredibly frustrated and very angry on a professional and personal front and almost 'freezing' in myself unable to know which way to turn. I was unable to move or to do anything due to the growing banks, courts and pension company's action. I have always been really positive in life and I still very much am.

I have provided a very clear sequence of my property

developing history shown in the Appendixes over four separate UK postcodes over twelve years. You can also see in the photo section evidence of Paul Keddy's excellent 'i' newspaper account of lending history which I was being affected by. I was simply in the eye of the banking *hurricane* tracking across the property developing *ocean*. My timing now in hindsight was matching the 'system' lending being pulled starting from 2015. The broker(s) set up the lending in personal names which was now being assessed as fraud as it was not in a limited company structure. Simple, the business was set up to put into a limited company but lenders and bridging companies wanted it in individual names effectively taking any protection away to protect their interest. They fully knew that and so did I and so did the investors and their lawyers. Hence why the attached Andrew Verity BBC article about the previous RBS Global Restructuring Group case which had involved the UK Bank of England Governor where RBS had given small businesses quote 'enough rope to hang themselves'. I had previously had enough rope to climb Mount Kinabalu, Mount Meru and Mont Blanc.

Building up from 2015 to 2020, as per all the media articles included in the photo section, it was clear as mud that the finance system was becoming just more restrictive to the point of have the wife, the kids, the homes, the incomes, the rents and all possible property assets, have everything, the cars, the pensions and whatever it took to get some funding even if there were restricted LTV's and in some cases at 170-270 times the UK base rate. Literally. Remember from before I had completely finished all my developments and in February/March 2020 we had about 98% full occupancy, then over the full 12 years of £7,850,000 GDV property developed and £522,000 per annum in gross rents in 16 months then after COVID-19 I potentially lost it all. On the books at least we do have the buy-backs and the supposed values in limited companies and the regulatory findings to come back. All is not lost just yet if the courts or lawyers could just reply or at least pick up the phone.

My real anger and frustration was that with all the 'huge' onerous security required, as soon as COVID-19 hit, the finance houses just pulled the loans. We had immediately asked for flexibility for forbearance and just 'help'. Absolutely not one piece of help or forbearance was forthcoming. The loans were increased by 45% and 75% respectively by both bridging companies to exit. No! Just pull the loan and crash sell for whatever the market would take. On paper that was about £1.1 million loss on GDV property values being crash sold and all involved fully knowingly that to be the case. Remember that the reserve price for 100 Lord Street was set to *specifically lose £850,000* on *one* building as recorded by Duff & Phelps for Together Finance. I remember speaking to the lawyer at Duff & Phelps who I will not name due to the investigation. I was incredulous as to why they were knowingly selling at a reserve potentially losing £850,000.

The manager had felt he was totally bullied by this lawyer especially over the rents which were totally misrepresented as were the building values. Once I knew their horrific fee structures I knew why. Lawyers in *three* hours could earn my military pension for the whole *month*. The fees for one 100 Lord Street lawyer to crash sell the one unit stood at £50,000 plus. This is a national disgrace for a building in the memory of 34 dead soldiers. No wonder they had such a terrible reputation. The problem here for them was that they picked on me. I was just the wrong man to do that to with my farm working ethos and with my Army and Navy Commando 'can do' military background. I was going to fight this now to the bitter end. Lawyers, courts, book publications, Parliamentary petitions, whatever it takes.

As one administrator has just stated, a contract is a contract. Houses sell for what they are worth at the crash sale time. He might want to explain that to the investors and the Legal Ombudsman to properties valued at £3 million plus equity. Like all the images of the Vietnam war and a soldier being killed the often asked question is *Why?* The case against *one* of my administration processes regarding Hatchard Homes Limited case 17 of 20 and John Paul Hatchard case 20 of 20 and *all* 11 companies citing possible 'fraud' with a simple question from myself of where has *all* the investor's money gone? You might all well ask the same. Together Finance and their lawyers Duff & Phelps can answer that as no one else can. Also ask Whitehall Pension and their lawyers JB Leitch the exact same question and with me being hospitalised in both March and May 2021. Even HMRC today. Why indeed? The Parliamentary petition is annexed to ask this question.

At this moment in time the authorities are telling me and the UK Nation that the high street retail commercial units have no value whatsoever. Zero. Really? I think the public really want to know this. Hence the Legal Ombudsman case and six other current ongoing regulatory investigations listed in the Appendix which I will come to shortly. Then add in to that the COVID-19 limited company evaluation process and 'system' querying the actual real market values of my limited companies now because of the Bounce Back Loans and grants. A new UK Companies Dissolution Act in the Appendix has just been produced in December 2021 and is now affecting the TM01 process. I am told by evaluators that COVID-19 has also now screwed up this process. So now properties, certainly those in the commercial sector, had no value whatsoever and the limited company group, which we had roughly evaluated at £1.5 million, potentially now had absolutely no value. I did not have the ability to run as a director anyway as I had given 51 investors 1% shares in each company. I had to fully declare the Assets and Liabilities to three underwriter brokers in roughly 2017-2020 i.e. they all had the same information give or take over £6 million of property assets not including life assurance and limited companies which would take the group to £9.047 million plus on the Assets sheet of the Assets and Liabilities as stated before.

The really pathetic situation was the other co-owner of the terrace buildings was effectively being 'blackmailed' and we had to just crash sell the whole portfolio. This was where an investor lawyer had altered her agreement compared to my original one supplied to her. This now really exposed the bridging onerous security in personal names and not in a protected limited company structure. This was absolutely key to what lenders had been putting onto small business owners as per the BBC investigation on the RBS Global Restructuring Group case and similar to the Norcross securities supplied.

Understandably that co-owner person just wanted to release those units fully to the administrator just to get out of the situation. Due to COVID-19 when the media hyped up the value of properties and the Stamp Duty Land Tax holiday the government then moved the date forward to 30th September 2021. This created a mini-bubble not helped by the fact that we in the UK did not have enough residential property anyway. Lawyers then got inundated so instead of taking six weeks for conveyancing they were taking on some cases that were taking *fourteen months.* Monetary interest was simply building up for the financiers and lawyers.

To add a final nail in the coffin, the terrace sales, despite the hype, all had immediate offers from approximately September 2020 but then took months to sell because no one was lending and lawyers in some legal practices were making more money from the COVID-19 misery of the above situation than carrying out normal conveyancing. For the record my own legal conveyancing team Dorothy 'P' has been the most incredible support to me over 12 years so my case against fee chasing lawyers in times of stress do not apply to all lawyers. Some are superb and do have incredible morals and ethics and the Law Society should be proud to have them unlike the other less reputable. There are good people. You have to find them.

There is now a Parliamentary petition for a government enquiry into SMEs and individual businesses and the treatment of people by banks, courts and lawyers during COVID-19 and the run up to it. I have now called on my MP, James Grundy, for a 100,000 signature petition here logged in the book appendices. It will be very interesting to see the legal hourly increase in fees and legal firms' profits made during and after the pandemic trading on dealing and profiting on citizens' misery. As a very good friend said to me, it has nothing to do with your business, it is what their agenda is and what money they can make. Today you don't need to go to war to take someones' assets, business, hard work and families off them. This is the 21st century, a new type of warfare. You will see later my approach to dealing with this.

Then a mortgage company threatened the terraces owner with administration because some tenants were not paying and at that stage we had a six month residential property government moratorium on access and evictions so we could then not market or sell. Remember the promise that all sales were to go directly to the administrator and not to me? Therefore I was unable to manage the cash flow. This also contributed to the damage of the portfolio and limited companies.

So in 16 months the 'business' had gone from circa £50,000 per calendar month gross income to £44 a day. We lost two charities because of this. It was worse commercially in July 2020 when the Government stipulated a nine month moratorium on evictions of commercial tenants. This was going from bad to very worse on a daily basis. This 'high average' soldier was now at the bottom of the class after 12 years of building up a very successful group of businesses.

Mindset

Friends who are close to me after being updated were incredulous and please note they were getting maybe 10% of the full horror of what was really going on during COVID-19 as my trying to explain in full just 'lost' some people. Some people just wanted the basics and some wanted war and peace. Then wisely in the summer of 2021 someone asked a very blunt question. 'Anyone sane would have committed suicide, what kept you going?' To note, I think in the UK the suicide and bank action bankruptcy rates are at an all-time high and personally at the time of writing in the 'fall' of 2021 I think it will sadly only get worse as the furlough ends and another lockdown looms.

I have tried to self-analyse the question I was asked. Three things come to bear on my mindset. These were being alone on the farm weeks on end, finishing the degree and completing my commission after the airlines. On the administration side, of all my 12 years of hard work plus our individual names as security and the fifteen years of marriage was about to be for absolutely nothing and contrary to all legal advice to just let the administration take all the remaining assets and maybe get 5% back to investors. There was no way in hell that I could allow this to happen. Investors' returns and the 'annulment' of my personal name and 'rescinding' of all my companies was now my very single-minded approach to achieve my mission. If I did not do this I could never ever face my ex-partner and children, my family and friends and my military guys again, as well as my clients and other business partners who had depended on me for years who would think the worst of me. I would have absolutely nothing, not even the respect of the children over what had happened. Other business owners might be happy to let it all go and let folk lose money but not me. Build up the case, be clear, be transparent and get the facts over and now you have nothing. Just get the authorities on your side, get book sales and publications out there and the media operations on your side with the petition. Ignore the threats and physical assaults. This is all about you now and only you who can take all this on and no one else. There were six clearly defined occasions where I froze and I just needed to undo the damage, reboot, repivot, get out of the rut, take on the finance system, the courts and the 'world' on – fully head on. 'Eat the frog' daily, it will be unpleasant but just get on with it.

I liked my own quiet company, as a young man on the farm, so weeks and months of being solitary during COVID-19 I could manage where others communicating online were all struggling. I could see that people's mental health was being severely affected by news from the main media outlets, COVID-19 and also social media content. It was so easy and clear to see. Finishing my degree was a simple no brainer after my parents' herculean efforts and was only an extra year of my life. The effective airline time and time away from the military was three years so this was a longer period to bounce back. At the time of writing since September 2019 and my own lockdown this next process might take another year to sort. These are the three experiences I think I used. Don't over think the process and just get on with it.

The main day to day technique I used during COVID-19 was a military course I attended. This was the RTI (Resistance to Interrogation) course also known in other countries as SERE (Survival, Evasion Resistance and Extraction) or CSAR (Combat Search and Rescue) training. A more popular interpretation of this type of training has been a TV series called 'SAS Who Dares Wins' where the participants undergo a watered-down version of RTI amongst the other physical challenges. Those who have viewed the programme will understand the concept of fierce interrogation techniques. It was set up for pilots and Special Forces and any troops who go behind enemy lines. It is a robust, tough and a very mentally 'odd' experience so much so that it is filmed and kept on Government files for 25 years I believe.

The course is a week long where you have a classroom instruction phase, then an escape and evasion section over several nights, then the capture phase involving a hunter force running into 'interrogation'. The evasion piece was ok. You had to map read and make RV's (rendezvous) carefully where there would be instructions for the next RV's and these sometimes involved vehicle and helicopter moves. Sometimes there was food and water like one single onion at one RV, showing that the Directing Staff at least had a sense of humour. Now with no sleep and having a large area to cover in the south of the UK near the coast you would be very hungry, tired and rundown but you had to be getting mentally ready for the dreaded 'beasting' capture phase. The area was extensive and you would pass by and look into some very large properties with families inside who looked nice and warm and were eating big dinners whilst we were freezing, cold, tired and hungry outside with psychologically a sign above us saying 'the losers'. Any thoughts of a farmer's hay barn with hens and eggs seemed very far away. Reality and TV are very far removed.

There was a safety piece where the Directing Staff had an armband and any medical or mental issues would be monitored and you could elect to come off the course. One Special Forces aircrewman did just this, they took his blindfold off and he left the course. It is an extremely unsettling and 'robust' course after all. I will come back to the class room phase shortly.

There is always a funny story. The onion was really foul and rock hard and made you get stomach cramps when chewing it. Also I was moving house and could only find a new pair of boots and therefore got massive blisters the size of golf balls on my heels. I ended up hobbling at the end plus my girlfriend at the time had just written off my car avoiding a deer the weekend before. The hunter force were paratroopers and my own two man team avoided them all throughout. At the next RV the Directing Staff with armbands said we were now 'captured' and so we were now moved into the interrogation phase and were bundled into vans.

I had been warned to try and get an idea of time to manage dislocation of expectation. Then it was stress positions, blindfolds and then very controlled shouting, engines revving, real dogs snarling at you and soundtracks of babies crying - the usual. It was the standard name, rank, number, date of birth, etc. answers that you had to stick to (this process has changed now). Apart from the vicious interrogation you are blindfolded all the time and I remember a female with strong perfume nearby. My interrogator was older than me, he was aged about 40 and sometimes there would be others with him - good cop bad cop. The interrogator left the room and left his sandwich and a cup of tea which I ignored despite not eating all week and was starving. After the naked strip search and the Directing Staff laughing at my blisters I could avoid another shouting match by simply leaving the food untouched. The interrogation was a welcome relief from stress positions as my back had been slightly injured previously. Get on with it 'H'.

Then the blindfold came off the next 'day' and a man with

an armband said ' Endex - this is the end of the course'. (Endex is a code word that means a military exercise is complete). You were individually debriefed and my guy was Royal Navy Chief Petty Officer who said I had done well. He said I should have taken the food and he said my name, rank and number were all ok except I had used my old Army number at first but managed to mumble something and use my new Royal Navy number. They were amazed at my machine-like responses and attitude then I mentioned the crashed car which was all I thought about during interrogation. They laughed at that. Finally you were invited to give feedback. Like the POW casualty rescue and terrorist rendition we did during the Iraq war this was all very strictly controlled. This was a very professional organisation indeed and the Directing Staff took it very seriously. The military is an amazing institution and sometimes resources abound in certain areas. So what did this have to do with the destruction of my businesses in COVID-19?

The RTI instruction phase was very interesting at the start. Without giving too much away, any military and indeed civilian live hostages are invited to debrief and many are filmed to then pass onto the UK RTI training courses to help troops fight, survive and win future conflict. It is exceptionally interesting watching them talk about wars and terrorists capturing hostages all over the world since WWII. So what did all this do for me in 2020-2021 and COVID-19 and the business world smashing into me? Well, I had also studied some of the US Vietnam fighter pilots and Special Forces captured by the Vietcong and one of my Royal Engineer instructors Major Carl 'S' had served in Vietnam at the end of the war. The stories were unbelievable with troops held for up to six to seven years in the Hanoi Hilton, the infamous POW camp and some were held in solitary confinement for *years*. It was incredible hearing their stories, how each day they coped with little food, the diseases, daily beatings and interrogations and how they each resolved to survive, win and come home. They were all ranks including Lieutenant Commander (later US Senator) McCain USN and Lieutenant Everett USN both fighter pilots who made the call that one day they would be released and come back to the USA. The latter went on to oversee the US Peace Corps whom I saw in Central America. When captured, what kept them going was their discipline and resolve to come home with integrity. It became their only mission.

On the TV films, when you see them on YouTube, they all have their heads held up high with pride even if they could not walk due to the beatings. I needed that discipline process for my own pride to deal with the destruction of my businesses and 'my daily mental beatings'.

I had then invented my own POW camp on site in Leigh, Wigan, in a small pokey one bed apartment with a desk, a shower, a sink and a cooker. My Hanoi Hilton was now Together Finance, Whitehall Pensions and HMRC. The 'bank' who pulled on my group and then the prison guards 'beating' me were the lawyers, a few very angry investors, builders, local drug addicts in my bins where the apartment was and indeed anyone trying to get money for free from me. Every day I was 'beaten' just like on the RTI Interrogation course. 'H' you just have to get on with it. I had a 'suicide watch' on me because of the Secretary of State of Business process on my personal administration and six assaults lodged with both Wigan and Dorset Police against me and some of my business premises and staff all of which are on record and filed with Greater Manchester Police. This was no RTI course, this was now very, very real. Physical assault did actually hurt me three times on site. I had absolutely no problem with that but the mental torture had the potential to really hurt me over a longer time. This was a tortoise and the hare story, it was a long game and not a sprint. I saw sprinters in COVID-19 fall by the wayside. Just keep going 'H'.

I wanted to come back from my 'COVID-19 war' and win with honour and integrity against the banks, courts and lawyers filing against me. Odd some may ask – for me it worked and got me through – the actual end result pending. I could go to the supermarket daily and see steak and avocado at Tesco and yet during COVID-19 our society was really struggling mentally, although it was hardly a Vietnam. For my equivalent of steak and avocado I ate baked beans and out of date cheap Iceland food. What I did get annoyed about at the start of COVID-19 was where you would be blocked at every supermarket entrance by case loads of gin and yet I could not get hand sanitiser for love nor money for my PPE business. China made it all. China made everything and it still does from where I am looking and with one million job vacancies in the UK, we make nothing or we make the wrong things.

Life is all about relative values. I could not let the side down. Seeing my kids 19 times for two days at a time in 24 months was not ideal but a lot of people during COVID-19 in the UK had separation, divorce, work issues, education of their children and the pandemic protocol to deal with. We were all suffering similarly. So just get on with it 'H'. Our parents turned out ok during WWII over six years with 67,000 civilian deaths compared to 150,000 deaths from COVID-19 over 16 months at the time of writing.

Anyway, I think I used a placebo that would maybe and naively mend my relationship. It neither mattered if it was going to work or not. What really mattered is the belief that it *might* - something, anything and sticking with it. I needed faith in something and someone. This quietly on my own was so very important. Also ignoring family, friends, investors, authorities, courts and lawyers who had a full agenda on me. I was very single minded to try and mend the absolute mess of the banks pulling the finance on me.

I was very upset at a family funeral at the start of COVID-19 where my little boy was distraught. He had not just lost a grandad, he had actually lost two men and a father that day because the man we buried had been all three to him. As I had been struggling with the business for years, this man had effectively stood in for my own father and for me too as a dad. My son worshipped that man. I was also for the second time in my life utterly heartbroken, now losing a lovely lady because of all this mess and if it took my lifetime to take on the banks and system, I vowed to do so after that very, very dark day. I was furious at the time over this.

We just cried in each other's arms right outside the church, me and my little boy and then his sister joined us. I felt so helpless to do anything. This was just not right or fair. I still worship my ex-partner and the ground she walks on. She is just an incredible woman. This was simply too much for one man to bear, let alone a whole family. This was my family who could never realistically put up with the continued restrictions on lending and then being smashed into and then suffering from the ridiculous pressure I put them under. My eldest was really traumatised over this whole business and I was getting text messages from investors threatening me and the kids. (These are all recorded for the police and doctor). There were also the bailiffs from Whitehall Pensions shouting through the letterbox and banging on doors. And they say they don't do this. Really? This made me exceptionally angry and I am a calm man. The real world, as Mohammed Ali once said, 'is a very tough and nasty place'. Get on with it 'H'.

Suffice to say the pressure on me as an individual was ridiculous even by my average standards. This inevitably impacted my family and my kids (remember how the banks and brokers and lawyers set it all up on the contract, setting up the security in personal names and not in the protected limited company structure) and for me that was totally unfair of me on the family. They all deserved medals from me for what they had to go through as well as the threats and abuse. I will not cover any more details to keep them safe. I hope the reader will understand this.

I hope I have been very careful in the book over family and friends as well as military names, references and security to ensure anonymity in business and any small future military operational security. I hope this is so for everyone involved. These include people who genuinely looked after me and in some cases brought me back safe and well. Several military folk saved my life and on eight occasions I nearly did not come back - that's what the military does to people. Nothing special - all troops are the same. Line infantry guys are in the line of fire in combat and you don't need to be a specialist to be facing a real deadly risk every day. They are real warriors, not timid, selfish, self-serving money grabbing people just looking out for themselves. Make money but do it safely.

For the unpleasant administration process it meant handing over everything or certainly the information on the Assets and Liabilities sheet. All bank accounts were frozen immediately which caused a problem with my £44 per day pension. This was the pension which effectively I had lived on away from the family for over 12 years for five to six days a week - which you can do, just! All I really needed was a working car (at the time of writing my car has approximately 150,000 miles on the clock and is 17 years old), a bed, desk, toilet and shower, a notebook, computer, mobile phone and internet. Remember pre-invading Iraq I only had my kit, weapon, body armour, my bed, my bergan (rucksack), food, water, mobile phone and a computer. The latter two were left on the ship and the Sea King helicopter was my 'car'. You don't need much of anything and as we moved though COVID-19 it has shown exactly what people, families and business don't really need in life. Strip it out for now.

The Secretary of State for Business representative's field agent who served the administration on me, Mike 'H' was in my office on site which had 11 incorporation certificates on the wall. He could not believe that I was living on £44 a day. Well, he was briefed on the accounts and was fully verbally briefed overall and the rest is now history. He was dressed smartly with a recording machine of minutes, like a policeman, quiet, deadly, controlling and overall generally professional. I even showed him all the three large buildings taken off me previously by Together Finance and their legal team Duff & Phelps at the forced auction eight months previous. On paper he seemed to realise what had happened. In my office four hours later, the field agent requested that everything was handed over, including proof of my hospitalisation in March and May 2020. On the record or off the record I thought I was being as open and correct as I could.

At this meeting, there were two things that were very disappointing, one being that I mentioned I owned a shotgun, and the second, the divorce. The latter was described as 'convenient', the former was noted and written down. This was totally unprofessional and it really annoyed me. Six hours later at my now ex-home the police banged on the door very late at night demanding the shotgun. It would have been nice to know that that process was going to happen since I had self-declared it myself anyway six hours previously. Then I realised that I had the shotgun certificate on site up north with me in Wigan. Just after, with immediate effect, I was put on a 'suicide watch' by both Dorset Police and Wigan Police and then by my family doctor in Dorset who received a call saying I might 'harm' myself. This was in case I apparently self-harmed or went and got another gun. Of note here 18 years previously I had in my last two years of military service been in Northern Ireland, Beirut, Iraq and Afghanistan supporting various 'specialist troops' on certain helicopter missions in charge of multi-millions of pounds of helicopter assets and weapon systems and effectively in charge of peoples' lives on my helicopter platform. Hero to zero at a stroke.

Now seemingly I was not fit to run a company let alone 11 limited companies and was now not fit for a firearms licence or drive a car having had speeding fines and parking tickets. Of note Wigan Council sent traffic wardens to local schools at 3.30 p.m. to give parking tickets to mums and dads picking up kids during COVID-19 after lockdown. This was totally moronic.

My family doctor, who was ex-Army, was appalled at the rather heavy handed approach by the police. Up until then I always had the utmost respect for them. I gave her an update and was told to hand the shotgun licence in as soon as possible after the administrator visit on the Friday meeting. On the following Monday, Tuesday and Wednesday I went to the Leigh town Police Station with people clearly on the top floor occupying the offices in a so-called remote 'unmanned' station. I had the shotgun licence, my passport and my driving licence and waved at the CCTV camera for half an hour for three consecutive days and tried to phone in on their emergency phones outside. I also flagged down two police cars where we locally had the Fat Sapper US style take out diner. They were too busy, quote dealing with 'domestic violence'. On the fourth day I drove to Wigan Police Station where eventually I managed to hand the shotgun licence in and this was only after I started filming on my phone camera citing a suicide watch which I had a civilian witnessing. Funny story. Amongst a sea of utter stupidity I got a speeding ticket going back!

Wigan local authority never supported my endeavours yet I had spent 12 years away from my family giving back after military service providing £6 million of newly developed property and housing families and businesses from completely empty abandoned disused units. As well as this I provided £1,485,000 of council tax and business rates for the authority to pay for police, NHS, fire brigade, military services and schooling - that was a lot of extra tax from one man. Now all this. It had become a total joke and it seemed I was a total laughing stock.

So it took me four days to hand the shotgun licence back. I am still under a 'suicide watch' today. Later I would recall similar access issues to the authorities at both the Yeovil and Wigan Courts. One last item here Fat Sapper, the take out, supplied free food for first responders to the fire, the police and to two NHS hospitals in Wigan Borough in both July and October 2020. These were on specific two to three day periods each, promoted and covered in two newspaper articles. Interestingly, it took two nights for anyone to come down from the fire brigade and police to take up the free Fat Sapper food offer. In Iraq, Northern Ireland, Beirut and Afghanistan we had crews often on immediate, 30 minutes, one hour and two hours' standby and certainly a Search and Rescue standby at sea at all times. Why were there such poor response times from the police?

The previously discussed SAS personnel helicopter rescue mission in Iraq took 12 minutes on to the target. If after 12 years of serving Wigan Borough I was about to throw the towel in there was a bit more in me yet. In the eighteenth and nineteenth century I would now be facing debtors' prison as in the TV series Poldark.

Part of the ongoing finance issue and your journey with me so far was the restricted lending, building up over the 12 years post 2008/2009. I have made comments throughout the book in *hindsight* of my growing unease on the system which in reality I really only sussed out in 2018/2019. I believe commercial buildings on the high street have worked well for the last 100 years, until Brexit, COVID-19 and the banks started using the internet and Amazon as an excuse. I believe that shops haven't been lent finance properly since 2015 and I think it all started after 2008 and 2009.

Our risk profile was that we had about two thirds of residential to one third of commercial mix and we had achieved roughly 98.2% occupancy for 12 years (during COVID-19 lockdown we had 92.3%-94.5% occupancy). This was not bad considering that at the time of writing in the winter of 2021, we now had some more movements out of the commercial units with tenants leaving. We thought this was due to furlough finishing on 30th September 2020. We had six limited companies in January 2020 and set up five more in early 2020 for the simple reason that commercially we had to fill and keep cash flowing in the retail premises and the rents being paid. The extra companies were to be entrepreneurial and at the same time occupy buildings for Small Business Rates Relief, have potential government support and also have the ability to trade. This, as previously mentioned, is how you fund a commercial property on *'supposed'* exit lending. The annual rents are divided by the 'capitalisation rates' expressed as a percentage given on an overall building valuation, according to the supposed professional RICS process.

Wigan Council courts and the authorities, I think in terms of administration functions, were vastly caught short and were in any case not fit for purpose. Of the initial grants issued at the start of COVID-19 i.e. £10,000 per business, that grant worked for four of my companies. Then the system just seemed to dry up when we were eligible for another three companies and three government funding phases for lending. In the next phase of potential grants we were then totally blocked over £4,000 per business and the 'open back up' grants of £6,000 for the all 11 companies. My MP is investigating. That was potentially £130,000 of grants not available, remembering what I had paid in over 12 years to the borough, Wigan Council, on our empty buildings which was nearly £1,500,000. We were then advised that our claims were fraudulent which we thought was them just delaying. It was indeed them delaying and they were on the local news saying that they were running out of funds. Greater Manchester had even lost their shares dividend in Manchester Airport because there was no flying. This was my old Flying Colours and Thomas Cook airline main base. Life in full circles again.

There was a Wigan Council 'egress' email system which was totally unworkable. To cut a long and onerous story short their claim was that my business leases were fraudulent. On checking the lettings agency as most small businesses they, not me, had used a third party template. Remember our Business Loan Agreements for our investors? This was exactly the same process. Wigan Council then contacted the solicitor of the lease company who had used the template. Throughout my years of working with them the lettings agent had been using this very same template with no issues whatsoever.

Then the solicitor practice said they did not know who Hatchard was. The lease on the letterhead had the lettings agency clearly addressed and their office sat 50-150 metres from the three main buildings with over 35 other businesses claiming grants. The other non-Hatchard businesses with the same leases all got their grants. I was genuinely furious. Why me again? Later in 2021, of the four grants we did receive from Wigan Council back in 2020, they then later claimed on *me* for 'extra developer fees' for two terrace houses which had been completed some twelve years previous. This was an extra £2,500 plus over the amount in grants we eventually received. Totally unbelievable.

This was obvious discrimination by Wigan Council to me. I then yet again returned this information when they went down the investigation process on *my* database and then found they were totally out of date on many of *my* units. *I* then supplied the correct information to the VOA (Valuation Office Appraiser) database giving them the up to date data! From central government and the widely publicised spat between the Prime Minister and the Metro Mayor of Manchester in mid 2020, £80 million went to Manchester apportioned to 15 boroughs including Wigan Borough. £30 million went to the police. Where was my business and grant support money? I paid for it over twelve years in the town on my developments, 200 rental units we developed and filled.

At the time of writing 13 non-Hatchard businesses moved out in 2021, all with £10,000 grants enabling new Range Rovers, time off and relaxed walks, a year off paid and for some holidays. They were hardly providing to the community in the borough for local businesses and services as my group had done. There I was running around like an idiot cleaning streets up from fly tipping and being shouted at for the mess of my bins that I paid for from local shop owners for the bins that I had provided at my cost, for the other businesses to then use and then me being threatened by the council for pest control fines up to £5,000! People were filming it all and defaming *me* to the Refuse Department, for example Jazz Hairdressing! This might seem to the casual observer unimportant low level micro stuff. However, on a day-to-day basis it was everything with no administration staff or back up to deal with it all. I had to do it all remembering the Vietnam POWs attitude to authority and my lost soldiers in the buildings that I had just had to give back to the banks.

For 16 months my Hatchard group just kept going and you have already seen the group list of our activities presented and what we had given to Wigan Borough in terms of local business support. This involved two years on site away from my family, maintaining the buildings, dealing with fly tipping, anti-graffiti measures, security patrols and teenager ASBO issues as well as serious drug problems. I was providing free meals for hospitals, the police, the fire services and six care homes locally with Wigan giving absolutely nothing grant wise in 2021 in the second two handouts of grant phases. For the Fat Sapper take out brand, I personally dealt with the refuse issues, the graffiti and security and even tried to get the grass cut. I had tenants who were being paid up to 12 months by Wigan Council because they were on furlough. I could not move them out or get access to sell because of the banks who were crash-selling on me and because Wigan had no other emergency accommodation. This was now utter madness and I was beyond furious yet again. I thought it was a nightmare dream and I would wake up out of it.

However, there is always a funny story in a sea of despair. In May 2021 Wigan Council decided on a 'No Mow May' as the bee populations were down. Funnily, I wondered what the bees had been up to for the last 14 months during COVID-19 on the 'no Wigan mowing' policy. In fact that authority in my mind had closed down fully anyway. Maybe the bees had been on holiday and were exempt over the airline industry travel ruling! These people must think citizens are just plain stupid. For balance, some Wigan departments have been good such as the planning department with David Rawsthorne, the council's principal planning officer, the build control department and the commercial property lease departments. Also some of the town regeneration planning teams, especially Lin Hogan as well as the local MP, James Grundy who has been of good service in 2020 and 2021 and the Metro Mayor, Andy Burnham who had opened all our buildings previously in 2015-2018. I am fair in my criticism and praise as I was on the farm and in the military. However, I was starting to fall out with this council 'system' and the COVID-19 excuse attitude big time. The local courts I also fell out with and fell foul of and these are now currently being investigated by the Legal Ombudsman on the whole regeneration and COVID-19 mess. One last rather unfunny piece with Wigan on our 12 years of 93,000 sq. ft. of developments was the £40,000 of grants received in May 2020, this oddly has now been surpassed by the money the Hatchard group now owes Wigan Council as stated above. This amounts to approximately £42,500 plus which includes 'extra development costs and taxes'. This is now being contested. Is this a greedy authority or the unluckiest man in business? You and I both know the answer.

Protect

OK, so there is lots of damage. To recap, we tried to keep the business cash flow going and also the so-called micro-businesses going. As one investor called them 'silly little businesses' which I took to be a good description. Three of the later limited company set ups were more entrepreneurial and speculative. There was a security, a recycling and an Amazon box delivery type business - these were just more for the names and the Intellectual Property Rights. I then went on the gov.uk website to check what businesses we could operate. There were activities such as car washing and disinfecting which were a very grey area which we could or could not operate and these activities also included take-out food. A 'maybe' for me then was a 'yes'. I wanted to work. Another business was started, hence the book's title, 'Fat Sapper' which was centred on a US BBQ 'Mom and Pop' style business based on the US Discovery channel programme airing in January 2020 called 'Undercover Billionaire'. I was intrigued with the 2020 pilot programme where a billionaire, Glenn Stearns, parachuted into another US state with $100, a cheap phone and a pick-up truck and had 90 days to create a $1 million business from scratch. From memory he started in coffee then ended up with a Ribs BBQ business which 90 days later was valued at $750,000. Two things from me, I really liked Glenn and I really liked the BBQ diner concept and how the USA limited company evaluation process worked. Like the British TV programme again, Top Gear, how difficult could it be in the UK?

One issue I had as soon as COVID-19 struck was the immediate and complete shutdown of the UK with the inability of businesses being able to plan. I also got the government COVID-19 protocol weighed off on what you could do and not do very quickly. At the start of COVID-19 we had quite a few apartments which had become empty so we put them over to the NHS emergency accommodation programme. In three weeks we carefully completed a full refurbishment on a family member's home to be potentially rented for Airedale Hospital from Barnoldswick. This build process, previously in Wigan with a dedicated team, would have taken nine weeks but instead it only took me three weeks. We had to pre-buy everything quickly as the tradesmen were too slow. There were three months of glorious weather, no traffic and absolutely no queues as most people were sunbathing or doing lots of sport which was really noticeable, certainly in Wigan and Barnoldswick. Let them holiday, I could get on with my work and I achieved more in six months than in the previous three years.

I then caught COVID-19 very quickly over twelve days and I had to isolate whilst still doing all the administration and paperwork from the bedsit. Virus Boy! Two hours asleep then two hours working on and off 24/7 for 12 days solid. I was totally exhausted and very achy but slept when I needed it. I needed a rest after the house refurbishment.

The take out, Fat Sapper, from May 2020 to September 2021 was a main effort. Additionally I had the legal issues ongoing with the forced sales from Together Finance creating so much damage on the original restricted loan which then affected the previous legal claim against Hatchard Homes. I found two local chefs and set up pretty quickly. What I found utterly incredulous was that in a town of 60,000 people, I could not find a commercial kitchen to use. In a five mile Just Eat radius, I looked at 60 kitchens, hotels, pubs, fish and chip shops, schools, bakeries, in fact anything. The problem I had was with 20 people who worked in the business, only three people had a car. I was as usual doing everything as always. No one was interested. They were closed down, scared of the virus, lazy, it was too much effort, or they thought it was going to last two months. It was very, very frustrating. One night I then missed a turn and ended up in a Rugby League club at Leigh Miners Rangers on a Wednesday. On the following Saturday, we were cooking burgers and ribs with a great bunch of can-do people. We stayed there until the lock-down protocol changed some ten months later and so we moved to a housing estate nearby. Thank you Christian and Paul.

Briefly, I used to get quite sad seeing parents in their cars on their phones and tablets whilst their kids were on the pitches playing rugby. I used to take free food and flyers down to them, telling them to go and get mud on their shoes, get rain on their coats and go and live life and be with their family on the pitches since I could not. I now knew what was really important in life. Oddly I got quite upset over this. I was missing my children.

One thing I found in a blue collar so called 'aspirational town', was either an attitude of 'we can do this' or 'no, it is too difficult'. In the military I just didn't ever question the leadership because it was always so good and never in doubt. When I saw horrendous leadership during COVID-19 in a civilian setting, I now fully understood that you needed the bad to really get the concept of what was good. A football game is an analogy, a game of two halves. Good people are superb and I have no time for bad folk or lifes' takers. It was that black and white.

Rather bluntly (and gladly so) someone about twelve months after the last big forced sale by the bank in September

2021 said to me 'you may now have worked for nothing for twelve years on property worth over £6 million. How do you feel now after 24 months of trying to keep the commercial rents going in 11 companies worth £1.5 million that they all now also might be worth nothing? Stop and think, you now have no control, no sensible cash flow and the food business is only breaking even. What is your plan?' His sage wise advice was to take stock, try to influence a legal agenda and get any loose ends sorted. Then put each workstream into boxes to contain it and not to complicate matters. Just simplify it and then work up and out.

In reality, over the 24 months when I started my own lockdown, I had started contacting the investors much more regularly, stating the progress and the limited company contingency plans as the finance was already clawing back. I also gave them as much information as I could such as the Asset and Liability sheets information, the updates on the limited companies and turnovers and so forth. As I thought around September 2019 there was already an issue with *UK finance* generally (not the same named *UK Finance* organisation which effectively was the former Council of Mortgage Lenders). I just did not know what the trigger was going to be until 23rd March 2020.

On the influential piece of advice, I had a very strong audit trail of purchases and sales of property and the rental income with both my accountant, Norton Tax and the conveyancing lawyer, FMGH in Essex and additionally the self-storage and coaching businesses. Additionally, the build and maintenance business and the coaching business trail were good. Based on the damage on Hatchard Homes, my dilemma occurred, as we have already covered, by a lawyer not serving papers or witnessing the delivery of such. The main issue now was against me and the Wigan Court action versus the DVT hospitalisation. I was having to deal with all this plus the £6 million of property lost and the loss of the potential lease equity of £600,000, and now potentially all the 11 limited companies with effectively a £1.5 million of evaluation value lost due to the bounce back loans, the grants, the pension company action and the HMRC.

One major item here on all the 51 investors' correspondence over several years and now legal cases with Hatchard Homes 20 of 20 and also JPH 17 of 20 was that it was now two legal entities, 51 investors, 32 plus creditors, effectively three courts of Wigan, Bath and Yeovil with no personal representation due to COVID-19 and a remote online zoom service with the utter inability to talk properly to anyone. Six regulatory investigations and audited references, four media outlets and I was trying to find any pro bono support. It looked to me with a sizable chip on my shoulder that this was in the favour of the authorities, with Goliath and certainly not David. It was not so much who was right or wrong it was who was allowed to speak. The MP is now helping and is questioning why none of the regulatory investigations have any power at all, hence the petition.

'Influence' that word again. Just like being on a drugs patrol in the jungle or looking from a helicopter surveillance platform, I observed that I needed to look at assets and resources with a laser (which we used on the Sea King helicopters) which were not mine or down valued. So I tried to think outside the box, get an investor witness and anything to help influence and inform. I thought I was right and the so-called 'system' thought they were right. From my studies, I did know that at the start of COVID-19 and in 2008 and 2009, numerous business leaders got damaged and were sharing what had worked and what didn't work.

One of the issues for me being ex-military was having faith in the six UK so called regulatory investigations. This has taken over 12 months to date with no real tangible results yet. The new problem was that the unregulated or bridging agent was allegedly not covered. Funny thing, that this so-called 'insurance policy' was now being 'voided'. I had from September 2020 to September 2021 a continuous feed of emails and references from and including the Financial Conduct Authority, The Financial Ombudsman, Trading Standards, The Citizens Advice Bureau, The Serious Fraud Office and the newer British Banking Regulation Service and the Legal Ombudsman who was also investigating the whole legal process against my group. At the time of writing one set of lawyers are stating that if the main home was used as security then it was clearly a regulated investigation. This was so clear for some lawyers. The Legal Ombudsman was now taking 13 weeks to answer emails, no doubt due to a huge volume of other legal challenges in small and large businesses. Luke Johnson, ex-Pizza Express, predicted somewhat clairvoyantly in April 2020 that there would be a huge financial and legal mess and forced administrations caused by COVID-19. He is a prescient man.

I also instigated a military media operations campaign using Your Property Network, the property investor 'go to' industry leader publication, the BBC, the Times and the 'i' newspaper. For balance, the UK media in general have been good. The articles by Andrew Verity at the BBC, Paul Keddy at the 'i' newspaper and James Hurley at the Times, which I have included in the appendixes, concerning small business finance restrictions over a number of years were all incredibly accurate and fed to the public mid 2021. This tied in with the Mike Norcross suicide report by the BBC and the associated Coroner's report dated July 2021 and additionally the older dated BBC 'RBS GRG' rather damming article on Corporate Finance giving SMEs 'enough rope to hang themselves'. I was a subscriber with Your Property Network having been a faithful reader for 10 years and I was trying to warn them over the financial restrictions to help other investors with my books and articles but they kept being put back from three to six months. I put the suicide watch on each media article as a header and was disappointed with the lack of any feedback whatsoever from some sources. I had a message and a clear mandate to the investing industry to say 'look what is happening with finance'. Was this ignorance, head burying or a threat that this could harm the property investing industry? I thought readers, coaches, mentors, investors and finance groups really needed to know. An ex-military chap was being strangled yet again supposedly fighting for funny old democracy and free speech but with the mute on everywhere you looked. I was getting frustrated again and I felt I was being pushed out and ignored and I felt very lonely. I just had no voice as an individual. People and business and the 'system' were continually smashing into me, something was fundamentally just not right.

The main issue I was having was that I was a single voice

doing everything on site, all the administration and trying to be heard by legals as well as trying to get a media article out as David not Goliath. Hence my writing of this book and my other '100 Business Lessons learned from Brexit and COVID-19' book – a sort of 'it does what it says on the tin' publication. Being able to influence and effectively whistle blow was impossible. I had no time to speak to the children, I was missing court deadlines through increasing illness, and everyone was working from home which I personally found either legally or financially near impossible as a one-man band. Over 30 emails from me to the administrator for Hatchard Homes with Grant Thornton were completely ignored, Wigan Court allegedly did not have time to open my files, Yeovil Court were not answering phones despite my three hours of calling over two days and media outlets were not getting back to me. The creditors and investor updates were late. The list of impossible items for any small businessman or woman goes on. David trying to even talk or get Goliath to listen never mind getting the first shot in was an impossibility. All this 'tech' communication and 'noise' and yet it seemed there was an innate inability to have a simple conversation with the right people. I now see with the administration process why even without COVID-19 it goes on for years and why the only winners are the banks, the lawyers and the courts. There you have it.

Adapt and Overcome You Must Win

I have gone macro above to give you the bigger picture and so I now want to go back to micro and look at the smaller details. Go back, re-invent, start again and simply go back to basics whilst the legal mess above ferments away.

The simple mission now is going to a Parliamentary petition with my MP. This was initially blocked as was the book and also the Government TM01 action was being blocked to hand back my directorships. That was all fine by me as long as I had an audit trail of me doing as I was told and what the 'system' was doing to David. Then I had to sell 200,000 plus books to get my investors' money back from the so-called UK non-existent finance system after twelve years of no proper or systemised UK commercial bank lending. I wanted to be able to influence the so-called financial, legal and governmental 'system' with a better way and another approach. Now with the aftershock of COVID-19 smashing into four million small and medium sizes businesses and individuals with loans and borrowing being called in it was time to get together a proper and detailed action plan.

I will mention here, we have technically and potentially arranged buy-backs on the three main buildings with a proper market value overall GDV of about £4.5 million on a 75% LTV mortgage therefore giving about £1.4 million of equity. That is if the administrators can be bothered or 'whether they sell the debt onto a third party'. The drive was how much money they could make. That was the actual quote recorded I was given and again it made me feel very unprofessional. I was also accused of lying hence I started to record everything.

So the ridiculous situation after twelve years was that now I was having to do even more work after building up a £6 million portfolio and additionally running 11 micro limited companies. This involved even more work. Much of this work consisted of trying to undo the severe legal and system damage and pay back investors by potentially buying back all the original development buildings. These included buildings which had been empty for ten years or more in some cases and that we had developed and brought back into use with bridging and investors and then fully rented out. To then have the so-called banks pulling lending out and for us to then have to buy back the buildings back out of administration with book sales and flipping burgers is just appalling. Is it me or does that sound like 'system' fraud or a completely dysfunctional UK commercial lending system? It is totally moronic, ridiculous and downright unworkable.

No wonder Jes Staley at Barclays in June 2021 laughed all the way to his bank when he said the banks will have a bumper end of year in 2021 with the booming UK economy. He then left that bank in November 2021 after the Epstein case. This lending action is a national scandal and there is nothing being reported in the mainstream news and in social media. I, the 'Fat Sapper', am now. Come on the media, we need you to step up to the plate, we need a small business petition to expose this for the benefit of society. Parliamentary petition Fat Sapper 'Go'!

I think the absurdity of the twelve years of my extreme hard work and all this occurring now is with me having to now write a 'warts and all' industry whistle blow exposure with a very personal story. And to then have to raise even more money as the banks pull even more money out makes for a totally farcical position to be in right now especially today as the Bank of England lending rate currently sits at 0.1% APR. This is the lowest it has been in 400 years and yet there is no lending for me and my businesses. Why?

So what? Recession, austerity, compliance and regulation,

Brexit and the COVID-19 eras, and may I venture, a post COVID-19 defined era? The landscape for myself in the last twelve years and for any future investing, certainly on the commercial high street in what I would call real world towns and cities, is now simply impossible. I think you will agree this makes for grim reading. There just has to be another way. Someone the other day said to me that you are very, very entrepreneurial in your approach to life. My reply is that I think this is absolutely not the case. Instead it has been in utter desperation to end up where I am today and this has been the same for so many other SMEs, property owners and business leaders. My experience of UK businesses and the UK commercial property sector frankly has been appalling in hindsight. The only reason I introduced my rather average farm upbringing and military career at the start of the book was to give the substance of a character just trying his absolute very best. Most military people would generally prefer to keep in the background which is the nature of the beast. I have not written the book for me, I have written this book for others who deserve better from me. Right here right now I actually 'loathe' the system, the banks, the administrators, the lawyers and the courts, and dare I say thankfully, a minute group of ruthless investors who are trying to damage me on the basis of expensive legal mis-advice. The truth will come out on a petition eventually for the good of everyone, especially my investors, and 'loathe' is a strong word. The books and the regulatory investigations will both bring into play the potential buy-backs as discussed.

'Most of the important things in the world have been accomplished by people who have kept on trying when there seemed to be no hope at all'

Dale Carnegie

22

Microbusiness: Keep Trying, Keep Small, Keep Flexible

On a different and more positive outlook let us have a look at the micro businesses instead to see the reality of what is really going on in the 'arena'. Some of my micro businesses were set up prior to COVID-19 and then some were set up in early 2020, at the start of COVID-19 and as the lockdown protocol kept changing. One main thing I saw on the news throughout 2020 and 2021 was the entrepreneurial spirit and downright focused mindset of small business owners to try anything, win, succeed or fail. These men and women gave it their 'all'. It was easy to set the COVID-19 society 'rules and protocol' up as a PAYE employee and be paid on time on the last Friday of the month but for four million SMEs and individual folk who had to fight tooth and nail for every scrap of money, cash, support and funds wherever, whenever, it was quite a different story. And this was at the height of the pandemic rules which were literally changing every week, every fortnight. On the battlefield you fight every day for every scrap you can get, ground, rations, water, ammo, fuel, intel, troop welfare and whatever you can find.

I think a lot of people reading were never really aware of the stress and the issues going on for many small business owners. It was heartbreaking to watch people in tears on YouTube closing down businesses after all their herculean efforts to get around the COVID-19 damage with regulators enforcing closure. In Greater Manchester in 2020, £30 million was allocated to Police and Enforcement, this is a lot of money for PAYE workers with overtime. For the record, the Police in many cases have been accused by some SMEs as bullying in nature in view of the courts and their actions.

The £30 million for police meant to oversee businesses and COVID-19 protocol which was fine but pay more to public servants with overtime but then a lot of SMEs missed grant payments and many were not allowed to trade and who suffered not being paid a regular wage.

On site I saw this at first hand. Haves and have nots. It was not a north, south, middle class or working class divide, it was PAYE versus small businesses who had absolutely nothing or who were barred from resources. We have, as part of this, had a society in the UK being divided gradually into two halves which has split communities and really caused divisions and conflict. How could we get around this? I hope the examples below give hope, light, another approach and some very anecdotal stories. 'Fat Sapper' has always traded in *'real politik'* and not theory. You can win, fight and survive if you want to.

Fat Sapper Diner BBQ: The Take Out Business 2020-2021

Fat Sapper BBQ (hence the name of the book) was set up because of the previously mentioned US Discovery TV programme which in January 2020 was centred around a US BBQ style restaurant diner on the franchise model and also the gov.uk website for the allowable business programme during the full lockdown. This allowed hot food take outs. We also needed to create rents in commercial units in the large, previously mentioned, 100 Lord Street, 123 Bradshawgate and Platt Fold Street units. For example Lord Street had the head office of the BBQ diner. It operated approximately from 1st May 2020 until closure on 30th September 2021. Headline figures showed a gross turnover of £139,000 over 14 months and it received a £10,000 grant and effectively broke even. It has been kept on using the brand name and this is why this book has the same name and will come into the plan later as 30,888 meals were cooked from £5 scratch.

I learned a lot here. I will give a potted history of the set-up of the Fat Sapper take out, the entrepreneurial mindset and how I just kept trying things. I asked for two chefs on the internet and found two people out of work. Over fourteen months we ended up at various stages with twenty people working for us with eventually four core people who wanted proper work. I had the vision for the business. Only three out of twenty could drive and that was a major issue in itself. In a northern UK ex-coalfield town in Leigh, South Wigan, with a population of 60,000, the Just Eat model gave us access to a five mile radius to eight local nearby towns. At the start of COVID-19 I tried *sixty* commercial kitchens in all the towns in the radius including pubs, hotels, shut take-outs, fish and chip shops, chinese restaurants, disused kitchens, churches, burnt out take away vehicles, indeed anything. Over seven weeks there was absolutely nothing. Businesses, people, partners and property owners were just not interested, lazy, anxious, or not bothered. To be honest I was pretty appalled by the apathy.

Then I got lucky with a rugby club where I did the deal on a handshake which lasted until they could open ten months later determined by the COVID-19 protocol. The kitchen was upstairs at the club so we were off the road and effectively this was a so-called 'dark kitchen', a concept where the kitchen was in a remote site off the main street. I set this up as a take-out with our own drivers. We were open six days a week and this stayed the same even when we had to move to a Wigan Council commercial shop tenancy on a housing estate when we had a week's notice to move. On that second location we went to a three day working week (open over the weekend). The days were reduced as paying for the drivers during the week and the weekday turnover was just taking money out of the business.

One of the main items for me was the owner, manager and worker mentality. I had the two chefs, one was ex-Subway and one was ex-Dominoes, the latter saying he had been in charge of £30,000 a week of turnover sales. We paid cash at the start so clearly tax was their responsibility. We eventually had two separate families with three to four people, all working several jobs with no real responsibilities, and again I just seemed to be doing everything. Some of these households had four incomes coming in as well as getting state support. For me the furlough went on four months too long. The system was paying people to stay away from work and I really struggled to get chefs, front of house workers and drivers from a population of 60,000. In October 2021 the UK had one million jobs vacant so workers had plenty of choice and because firms did not have enough workers this started to cause wage inflation and pressure amongst suppliers too. During COVID-19 the pressure was on the shoulders of the owners and not the workers who could simply come and go as they pleased.

Those who owned cars and those who didn't I felt was important as those with cars were driving unnecessary errands ordered by young people who were not car owners. The young people who had not owned a car before did not understand the costs of poor stock taking and thus having to buy from the expensive corner shops instead of the main food suppliers. This is very basic common sense.

Another mistake I made was that in the military everyone was mission focused from the General and Colonel down to the Trooper or the Sapper. In the take out business it was very obvious most workers were only there for the hourly rate cash which was paid weekly and they were not there for anything else. These workers and one of the so-called managers were not really bothered whether we did black milk shakes or square pizzas. One of the managers in hindsight was not manager material and had a drug and gambling problem and towards the end was stealing off the business as the EPOS (electronic point of sale machine which helps stop petty theft) magically kept breaking. Getting motivated young staff to stay off a mobile for an hour was like pulling teeth. I could even see anxiety in the older if they did not get their 'phone fix'. The town does have a serious drugs issue and will be similar to many other 200 towns in certain areas in the UK. We found that you could smell the drugs in the street when making deliveries.

I would say that 90% of my workload across 11 limited companies was with the worker issues in the food business. I would often have agency drivers who were so incredibly unreliable. In contract you would look pretty stupid on the battlefield not turning up and in 18 years in the military I never looked over my shoulder. In the civilian business world and certainly post pandemic I now trust absolutely no one. I hope my attitude here is short term as on the whole, I do like people. Chefs were the same and people would leave with no notice at all despite a two week notice period. The teamwork was just not there. I did find that the older people were better generally and we did have natural leaders coming out to help with ideas because they were parents who had some responsibility and were just more mature. These guys naturally came out under pressure. One of the managers I had left with no notice, I believe it was because the natural leaders had exposed him and they could see him for what he was. The next manager really took up the reins and he did exceptionally well as did the core team.

Those are a rather blunt series of observations through different phases of COVID-19. Folk in the area were OK overall and our customer base included well off families in better towns, office and construction workers and students and mid-age teenagers.

One positive thing I learned was that so many small and

medium sized enterprises and 'Mom and Pop' businesses subsidise failing businesses from their own money or from their partner's money. This is also very prevalent in the USA. I was doing this in Fat Sapper due to having a weak manager and also the COVID-19 challenges. This was certainly the case pre COVID-19 and very much post COVID-19. Owners just cannot afford this situation and I can see the same in the USA. Examples of inflation in the UK, starting in the autumn of 2021, are Royal Mail rises at 12%, my conveyancing solicitor 15%, fuel 52%, minimum wages increasing 10%, insurance premiums 25%, new Blockbuster cinema film tickets 20% and the Nationwide House Price Index increases of 12% annually. In 12 years we hardly raised rents yet landlords and landladies are portrayed as pariahs in the press. I also have a so-called 'shutter index' measure based on how many high street shutters are closed daily. I am, to the most part, essentially based in South Wigan and on the main high streets there are at least 100 out of 476 businesses which are currently shut. This is a lot and I think more are yet to come.

On the micro side of hot food take out was the continual need, almost daily, to adapt. Just Eat and local walk-ins would normally be 75%/25% split but would vary. We eventually moved to a housing estate which worked at just above break even, even after we changed the week to the weekend model. It was a very poor area with little footfall but no one else would give up a commercial kitchen or be bothered to open or do joint business.

Over 14 months I oversaw all sorts of trying absolutely anything. In May 2020 we provided outside tables which permitted a pedestrian access licence which Wigan gave out for free. Every month we offered a special event where we promoted Valentine's Day, the Football and the Euros, Mother's Day and Father's Day, 4th July American Independence Day and so forth. We had an ice machine, waffle machines, a popcorn machine and posh coffee using a domestic £200 machine not a silly £4,000 commercial machine on contract. We had a local lady who made us nice cakes and would make Mother's Day cakes and so forth. We produced big breakfasts, ribs and gorgeous 28 day mature beef, Sunday roast beef, pork, turkey and gammon, burger meals and proper food. I gave up trying to gain an alcohol licence from Wigan Council as even the Hygiene Food Licence took over a year to get. Why so slow? It was ridiculous. They were using COVID-19 as an excuse every single time. Staff would never clean the outside areas or pick up the litter but would watch me while they were on their phones. I would clean up the graffiti and clean up the park on Saturday mornings to make it nice for the local mums and kids and to market the business. My team posted this on local Facebook, Tik Tok and Instagram. Additionally I posted leaflets throughout almost the whole town and made 30,900 meals during COVID-19. Encouraging workers who wanted to get fit with steps on their phones by paying them to leaflet was a good idea but such a job was looked down on and I ended up with only two out of twenty people who I could trust. I also did it myself and got fit and delivered 50,000 over six months.

We supplied free meals to the two local hospitals, six care homes, the police, the fire brigade and the ambulance service and additionally we helped a Veterans group. I found this worked well where we were continually giving but it was a balance of a commercially viable enterprise and giving, as the hand that fed was often bitten off by greedy people. In a COVID-19 society or a local town wanting something for nothing, local business cannot last on this business model. I tried everything but it was normally always me initiating everything, although my last manager with support from others, was starting to get better over time. The later manager to his credit started to take on the accounts, managing the cash cash and sorting out the wage roll and this was a welcome relief. He actually understood business and profit.

One last observation and advice is to get rid of people who keep saying yes. They would come up with ideas and put them to the poor manager who would say yes to them and then do nothing. He had no idea about money and business but just kept saying yes. You need these poor experiences and poor people to then know and learn where you truly are with your team. You then realise that you have good people and a good business. It is very refreshing when things go well. I also noted I would struggle to pay for a new machine and then the staff would ask how it worked. My reply to them was to take the initiative which they would do eventually. We had about five extra new food type product lines but as soon as I was away (this happened rarely) the staff would switch off lines on Just Eat. I could start to monitor this remotely. They would then not do waffles or popcorn, they would not cook what was difficult and just switch the Just Eat availability off. This was absolute laziness and I would have to be chasing them up all the time. I was paying a manager wages to do better than this which annoyed me. After years of my always being on time now the deliveries could be very late. Sunday lunches and on a busy Saturday night you might expect up to an hour's delay. Sometimes the guys would be so late on food times but they just didn't seem to care about it. It was the continual monitoring that takes so much energy, time and effort. Mobile phones and the attitude to work really affects business productivity and my faith in people and work and business really changed over COVID-19. This attitude to work will come back and I see why immigrants always do so well. They fight for everything. They have hunger and do not have a 'welfare will pay' attitude to life. It is a tough call by me but so is the 'bottom field' on Commando Training and rescuing 56 seriously injured soldiers. I was hungry for success. I would try anything. Often unskilled people would really try my patience too and for many I don't think they had any realisation of what I was trying to do for them and the local town.

The secondary location and poor footfall despite the Just Eat 'dark kitchen' remote site concept was an issue. The other real main issue was worsening ASBOs from the local teenager groups with many dressed in £400 outfits which included expensive trainers and expensive phones, taking taxis wherever they went. They were drug pushers for the county lines and this was very noticeable. This just added to my increasing frustration caused by exceptionally poor policing, drugs, lousy discipline and no parental control. Additionally large groups would descend into libraries, restaurants and pubs making a nuisance of themselves during lockdown and not adhering to social distancing. Crowds of 100 teenagers would just congregate. I realise as an owner this must come over as me being really grumpy. I had twelve years in the town developing properties and trying to rebuild and this took a huge work ethic. I don't think the workers realised or were bothered at all that the high street commercial lending depended on crime statistics, drugs, employment levels, policing, refuse collection and school performance. Car insurance was high in the area for a reason and throughout COVID-19 none of the leaders seemed bothered at all.

I then assessed the Fat Sapper take out business and planned rises of 5%-12.5% on VAT, people coming off furlough, the legal TM01 action on the companies and antisocial issues on the estate along with very poor policing. It would now be wise to stop and hand the hiring back to the council. Making a big full stop business decision is difficult when it has been your baby for so long but immediately I could sense the huge weight off my shoulders. It was a very nice feeling and the sales handover and walking away was remarkably easy. Just do it if you need to.

This, rather oddly, proved to be a very good thing. I was not continually having to subsidise from elsewhere to make any shortfalls and additionally was not having to drive on Friday, Saturday and Sunday. I could get my time back on more valuable and more important activities. We sold all the movable chattels quickly and made £1,000 which took care of the final payroll. One last item was that I was threatened, oddly enough by the sacked manager chef, who went on to social media to damage me wilfully and his co-workers saying he wanted Fat Sapper to fail. Therefore, in a good way I really wanted the brand to continue and succeed hence the book title to keep the name going. We assumed he had been found out on his drugs, his gambling and theft by our team hence his abrupt leaving. As they say in Yorkshire 'nowt as queer as folk'. To prove him really wrong I wanted the 'Fat Sapper' book to take on the banks, courts and legal action exposure and win by exposing them and then get self-perpetuating cash flow from the book sales. This in turn would enable better sites and restaurants in the future plus finding better people to add to those few good guys we did have.

When we left and closed the site we often had local kids aged about six to ten with no parents around. We would get them out of the rain and sometimes feed them for free. They were really good kids despite the estate's reputation. They all came to say goodbye to us - some of the younger ones were crying. The community was sorry to see us go. My good manager's two children and his partner spent a lot of time on site and they always smiled when I turned up. Up to this point I had seen my own kids 19 times in 24 months like so many others during COVID-19. I remember servicemen and women who could do six, nine or as much as 12 month tours away from their families.

'Fat Sapper': The Man Who Took On The Banks, The Book 2021

The main mission of this book over my twelve years in business and in property with nearly £8 million of property development, over £522,000 of gross annual rents and 11 companies from all the evidence supplied is because it has become abundantly clear that UK finance in the mixed use and commercial property space had eventually become totally unfit for purpose and had just ground to a halt. The Government Parliamentary petition at the rear of the book amongst other things is to whistleblow a supposed finance industry to admit to the whole of the UK public that all shops and retail on the ground floors in every town and city have now zero value. Therefore having trillions of pounds sterling in property values wiped. If this is not the case then the Government authorities should seriously do something about the underwriting. Pensions are lodged on commercial units. It has also been the same for small SME 'Mom and Pop' type single shop units and any form of supposed business lending to individuals. The Bank of England base rate has been sitting at 0.1% APR - 0.5% APR, the lowest for 400 years yet there has been no lending or only lending with onerous extension charges and multiple securities including families' homes, assets, pensions and cars. Again the BBC Mike Norcross suicide report really highlights this in the extreme. Some administration lawyers are saying openly that this is not widespread. Let the Parliamentary petition sign up numbers prove this wrong.

The rather blunt aim of the book was based on the experiences of two people I have read about. General Ulysses Grant who helped win the US Civil War in the 1860s and then went on to be President of the United States. He then lost his money in an investment scheme and wrote his memoirs with Mark Twain marketing the book about the Civil War and retrieved his fortune back that way.

Likewise, a more modern example of writing a book was Bob Mason and 'Chickenhawk' based on his experiences in Vietnam as a helicopter pilot after he fell on bad times and then wrote the book. When I last looked it had sold over 500,000 copies at $20 each - you can work out the maths on that. As a small addition, the book 'Soldier Five' is about an SAS patrol in the first Gulf War that I was also very interested in due to the legal aspects of getting Mike Coburn's book published. The authorities tried to ban his publication as this book was by the lawyers. There is conflict in both war and business.

Two things that impressed me about these men was the entrepreneurial flair to be able to turn failure into a glowing success. The secondary benefit was that it shows the human spirit of when things are down some human beings can really turn things around. I hope you have felt that with this book.

I wrote a very successful, easy to read, business book called '100 Business Lessons learned from Brexit and COVID-19'. It does what it says on the tin. This book, 'Fat Sapper', was potentially legally blocked by several lawyers because of the whistleblowing of the whole system. And to one lawyer who queried where sales were being deposited, I politely explained that the proceeds will go to the investors.

'Bright people can invent a brush but don't know how to use one'

My father

Covid 19 Busters Limited 2020

Another microbusiness set up with the pandemic was

'Covid 19 Busters' based on the film Ghostbusters. This was a light hearted business name for dealing with the virus. Like so many others I wanted to provide masks, gloves, sanitiser, office screens and any other associated items on a 'try and see if it works' type basis.

The unexpected major issue was the actual company name. 'It is a scam, it will give you the virus, the testing kits are illegal, the people behind it all are not qualified' etc. at the local level. These accusations or views are just part of business life. I manned the shop daily from 10:00 a.m. to 16:00 p.m. and you could physically see people walk away thinking the place was infected. Once we had delivered leaflets and used social media people eventually accepted us. I was genuinely surprised at the initial reaction.

At the macro level it was much more serious. Companies House, Wigan Council, URL, Paypal, Izettle, etc. all had issues. In hindsight I probably should have used another name, anything but with COVID-19 in the title. It took quite a long time to get all the landing pages and the 'system' to accept it. Wigan Council were trying not to pay any business money and queried the name and dates. Thankfully I had someone who had set it all up so we had a trail of authenticity. Wigan Council were not helping yet again.

Back in March, April and May 2020 if you wanted to get drunk on gin in the UK you were fine judging by the entrances to most supermarkets. However, as for hand sanitiser it had to be via our Chinese cousins as no company in the UK made this in any volume. From memory I think we used 'Made in China' and I must admit their emails and their attitude to customer service would put any British citizen to shame. They were geared up, smart, sharp and immediate. For me, at the same time, the UK produced no PVC, hand sanitiser, gloves, masks, cement, plaster and so forth. Indeed we made nothing or anything. I mention the building items too, as at this time I was trying to get building supplies, as for that industry there was annoyingly no lead time from the Government to get supplies in before they shut.

Back to Covid 19 Busters again. I tried to get people to help but, again the worker mentality, the lack of leadership and initiative and also that many workers did not have a car really restricted me from doing business. The main mission was always cash flow and having to let out a building for the dreaded commercial lender again.

I got the basic items listed above and got an airbridge delivery set up (an airbridge is the route and means of delivering material from one place to another by an airlift). I found basic supplies and an enterprising entrepreneur in Glasgow so I had a tertiary supply chain. I then found a wedding dress maker who could make nice whacky designer cotton face masks. Helen was really good. Extra products included a resourceful South African builder with a car battery size ozone cleaning machine, which could sanitise larger items like trains, cinemas and hotels on a hire or buy commission basis. I thought this would do well but it had no real take up. He left a device onsite but in hindsight it was probably just too expensive for the locals. Eventually someone found me a gin maker in London creating sanitiser so that worked. I was really enjoying the entrepreneurial aspect in the months of April, May and June 2020. There was nice weather, no traffic and in all the 11 limited companies there was huge variety. People were just so relaxed in the town and it felt like a holiday camp. It was totally bizarre. I was working my heart out which was a good thing and there were no traffic queues and so keeping things like Covid 19 Busters supplied was not impossible.

During this time I was also monitoring the gov.uk site seeing what businesses we could operate in each shop. I additionally supplied detergents and also food parcel boxes. I also had an education section with posters and YouTube clips as there was so much anxiety and worry over COVID-19 locally, understandably so in hindsight. The Izettle machine (machine able to take credit and debit cards) and going away from coinage was a big issue from memory for the locals.

The testing kits were also a big issue, like the company name, and were very scam orientated. This was to the point that the authorities threatened to shut me down from the upstart. This was the Wigan authorities again with their 'please help businesses' attitude. I did quite a bit of research here and sent off for a registration form trying to enrol a retired doctor to get involved with the testing kits and validate them. This flurry of activity then all seemed to calm down as every man and his dog was doing this. This was the same with the NHS emergency accommodation. Well done to all UK citizens who offered this. I was effectively driving every night at the takeaway Fat Sapper and then working daily in the Covid 19 Busters shop. Having the discipline to set up the shop daily helped my mental approach and routine. People were getting very nervous as COVID-19 progressed and I was incredibly careful with my hygiene on all of the projects.

As before I lost 12 days in early April being bedded down in my bedsit apartment but managed to get a lot of administration sorted. Accommodation, self-storage, the take out Fat Sapper, Covid 19 Busters and the car valeting and disinfecting business meant involving a huge number of leaflets for advertising the businesses. I had a local printer employed to print 2,000 flyers weekly which I would then fold and deliver most of them by myself. I saw Domino's Pizza was the only other company leafleting. Then a really reliable guy, Anthony, helped me later in the summer after I had been doing this for four solid months. Anthony had a brain and could take the initiative. In hindsight Fat Sapper, the take out, had a shelf life especially as the town was reopened but then shut back down as we were put into lockdown again. We both at the end got to a breakeven point where the sales just about met his wages.

I think we sold 11,988 sets of PPE masks, gloves and sanitiser overall. I offered some to care homes and hospitals as it was free marketing to help promote the business. We used Atlas Plastics for the office screens and they sold well. They had had a big order of shop and office screens that was cancelled from Paddy Power Sports Betting for their shops so we bought these as a job lot at a reduced price to sell for Covid 19 Busters. They also had a virtual printer for making proper face visors. Like all Hatchard products and services we did everything properly whether it was our property, food, cars or providing PPE. People would go and buy a product cheaply and then their cheap, badly made order (the majority of the time being from China) would be delayed. We did well here picking up extra trade. The PVC maker was really struggling with getting raw material supplies as everyone was in the UK.

The wedding dress lady did well on making the hand

made masks for adults and kids and later I looked at vending machines because of the cost of labour. I tried all sorts of venues but the local 'mafias' in the hospitality industry in the town were wasting my time by creating endless problems. After that we just stuck to the three main sets of PPE plus visors for hairdressers and office screens. Then, we went into the second lock down and by then the crazy China air freight prices had subsided and most folks now had their own supplies at home anyway so it was time to cash up. I donated a large set of sanitiser to a church and we made up PPE sets for Fat Sapper meals which worked very well to promote the take out business. Trying to bring businesses together was much like bundling the leaflets for each business to save time and cost.

One final small observation was the local behaviour in the high street shops. At the start there was nervousness on cleanliness hence the Izettle machines. People would come into the small shop and take photos, say nothing and walk off, and I think they were trying to then go and find the products cheaper online. Others would come in and try to get the prices down. I was always prepared for the questions like 'well I can buy those for x and y'. My reply was that the USA, FDA and UK NHS kite marks were a set quality which I was picky about. They all just wanted cheap rubbish. They would then show you on their phone and I would then politely show them the US dollar conversion plus the air freight costs and advise them of the four week delivery window. They would then leave and in three days they would come back and purchase.

I had two sales staff. One was a young girl who was behind on her rents and who was totally useless. She could not sell an ice cream to a school of kids in the desert as she had no intelligence and no sales initiative whatsoever. She was a local just wanting cash for no return. Anthony, on the other hand, was just fantastic. He was a nursery worker on furlough. He got into social media and progressed to the accounts. He also started to monitor the food and the car business. You will see below that he sensed my growing frustration with the local attitude to work with 'the really cannot be bothered workers'. He was absolutely one of life's good people.

Big Blue Self Storage (NW) Limited 2017-2021

Big Blue Self Storage (NW) Limited was an existing business in the Platt Fold Street large blue warehouse. It was basically 32 storage units, all of different sizes, from hut size, to triple garage size to large garden size. Going back to the development of this building we created more units by adding the mezzanine floor. The mezzanine floor had small domestic storage pods upstairs and larger more commercial units down below. One small change which we added later was a car cleaning business which we squeezed into the entrance. I will cover this properly under Centurion Car Valeting later. The business rates with the council would become an issue here. Wigan Council Valuation Office Agency had no idea about business rates on anything up to the time of COVID-19. They certainly do now after the grant fiasco when I found out they were completely out of date on my units.

Centurion Car Valeting Limited 2019-2020

Centurion Car Valeting Limited was set up in late 2019 to early 2020 on the back of one of the delivery drivers for the

I now had two workers again unable to drive and to cover this work. Unbelievable.

One last item was that I wanted to do car sales and car hire. One of the workers I hired was supposedly a 'real car guy' who then found a 'great deal car' and against my better judgement I took this on. My own business model was to work with older age Audis A4s and A6s to be serviced, have their tyres cleaned and so forth and make them roadworthy for blue collar workers as sales or hires. This particular worker then decided it was all too much like hard work. I ended up getting a gearbox, fixing it, MOT testing it and then servicing the car myself to make the numbers work. The £300 project ended up at £1,860. Some expert! In the end it worked well as I set up a deal with the new manager at Fat Sapper. He rented the car off me for 12 months and then bought it off me. I eventually made £1,000 profit, it helped his wages and it was a good car project in the end.

To finish this saga of the car valeting. The key issue was the 'attitude to work' mentality. Even after 12 years I seemed to be doing everything again when I just wanted someone else to take the lead. At 22 Engineer Regiment I was Cadre Officer, responsible for taking young troops through their first promotion levels including skills in weapons, engineering, bridging mines and soft skills such as bank accounts, public speaking and taking the lead in medical emergencies. All these troops were superb. They could take the lead and get stuff done anywhere in the world whether in peacetime, terrorist operations or in war. It was about people wanting to get on and to succeed.

In the car valeting business I had two guys in their 30s

take out, Fat Sapper, stating he knew someone who was a car and valeting so-called expert and who wanted a rental space. I had a look at the numbers and knew we could get more rent rolls into the large Platt Fold Street warehouse at the entrance. Centurion Car Valeting was rejected by Wigan Council for a grant with, as usual, no reason. The stock and machines cost about £1,500 and they set up a charge rate from about £7 to up to £60 to hand valet cars with two men on site. They were the industry experts and again I checked to make sure we could operate within the gov.uk 'acceptable businesses' website. Wigan's interpretation of the gov.uk website was a bit grey to say the least. I went down the route of disinfecting and therefore we cleaned and disinfected 2,700 cars during the period including site trucks, school mini buses and taxis.

Again I seemed to be doing all of the administration work. I was leafleting and trying to find more contract work, creating outdoor waterproof signage and putting sign boards up. I gave the guys at Centurion Car Valeting the advertising leaflets but every time I went to the unit the leaflets were still there. I then took them away to give to Anthony whom I could trust.

I managed to get more reliable contracts but I then realised we needed a small van to become a mobile unit so we would be able to cover a five mile radius. One of the drivers had a drink driving issue and had lost his licence and Wigan were delaying his reissue. Why lose it in the first place? The other driver then decided he did not want to do food delivery and that his car was unsuitable to take cleaning items. I offered my own old Audi but the delivery driver then said he wanted t stay on site. I had actually arranged two garage contracts. '

and 40s and I was not sure about them wanting to make the business a success, it seemed to be all just about them getting a wage. One had anger issues and broke a door and expensive equipment and I felt that drugs were an issue. The other had a drink problem, the proof is still on my phone. Anyway I had it all set up and wages were paid on Fridays. I worked hard to make it happen offering them free Fat Sapper food to help them and I tried to top up their wages. They then fell out. One left but then came back and ran his own business for a month. I paid the rent to get him going and you guessed it… he walked off site again 30 days later because his rent was in arrears. I never got the rent money back. Both were also on full welfare.

This would have been a great business as so many businesses had stopped during the pandemic and it was there for the taking. However, there were no drivers and now there were drink and drugs issues alongside the usual anger and anxiety issues. This was a town of 60,000 people and yet there were no workers wanting to work.

Boost 307 2017-2021

This was a training and mentoring programme which was set up several years ago in a Regus office which was numbered 307 hence the name. There was a drink called 'Boost' and as I have an interest in cars and aviation and they need a 'boost' to get more power the name seemed ideal. Also the number 307 had a Far East connotation for completeness, wholeness and synergy from research so it matched well. You have to check these things.

This mentoring was mainly concerning property and

business coaching and mentoring for small and medium enterprises. The property mentoring ranged from small buy-to-lets to Houses of Multiple Occupation (HMOs) and commercial property. The model was based on three days during the week mentoring and then three day weekend courses from Friday to Sunday. The mentoring of one to two students was a very good package and I did this for a third party company. They included genuine good value. It involved teaching, on site property viewings, setting up a bank account and a limited company, plus providing a so-called power team which included lawyers, surveyors, a team of property sourcing agents, insurers and the like. We would normally assist the clients in their time after the mentorship and help with their area visits all around the UK, in Scotland, Wales, Cornwall and London. At the peak this turned over £115,000 annually.

What was rather ridiculous was that our overseas clients, once they were finished in London, had to then fly up to Glasgow at their own expense to open a business bank account as we had managed to get just *one* bank branch manager out of 345 lending institutions to help. This was an RBS branch based in Glasgow, one out of the whole of the UK, and then a colleague, Kate who took it on over several years, helped to open over 1,000 accounts. Eventually as this was being run from south west London we managed to get a few other banks and branches to support the overseas clients but it was not easy. This was in 2018 and 2019.

One final note here, there has been a theme throughout the book about the damaging actions from banks and finance houses on business in the UK as per the Andrew Verity BBC article and especially the GRG investigation piece about Royal Bank of Scotland involving the new Bank of England Governor's investigative role. The Flying Colours airline I used to fly for started with seven planes and ended up as Thomas Cook Airlines with 34 aircraft. They were forced into administration by RBS bank. From rough memory Thomas Cook airline and their sister company airline Condor both required approximately £200 million each to keep operating. Condor achieved their loan helped by the German government and German banks whilst RBS in the UK declined and put Thomas Cook airline under. It then cost the administrators £140 million to repatriate all the passengers stuck abroad plus £60 million in staff wages to conduct the administration i.e. the same £200 million originally needed to continue and prosper. The reason apparently was they were paying PPI claims instead in the month of August, the same month that the airline needed to draw down funds. What did that politician previously quoted say, 'F … business'. Well RBS certainly did that to Thomas Cook and eventually our overseas clients. Together Finance and Whitehall Pensions then did the same to me. This is pending investigations now.

At the end of 2018 RBS then asked that all the limited company accounts that we had set up for those 1,000 plus clients be closed down, apparently because EU competition laws stated that RBS had too many business accounts. And I thought we were leaving the EU? I struggled through COVID-19 to set up business bank accounts and remember the fact that Together Finance and all other unregulated lenders stipulated that loans had to be in individual names, not limited company names. No protection then and onerous security and the inevitable COVID-19 financial failure. I even tried in 2020 to open a Lloyds business bank account which was denied. They are now the biggest private residential landlord in the UK. Funny that.

On the Boost 307 business side I had 440 direct clients and had presented all over the UK and worldwide in Singapore, Hong Kong, Sydney, Adelaide, Perth, Melbourne, Paris, Stockholm, Oslo, Copenhagen, Las Vegas, Bangalore, Dubai and Finland. In all, I mentored and taught about 2,000 people. We had set up over 1,000 business bank accounts and clients had invested the best part of £50 million plus in property in the UK. This was based on brownfield regeneration turning empty disused properties into habitable buildings from small terraces up to churches and the like. The annual turnover of the coaching in its prime year was about £115,000 gross. Sadly I was asked to leave the third party business at the end of 2018, six weeks later they went into receivership with a $100 million per annum turnover. My comments about using premium economy vice business class at the time obviously fell on deaf ears. What did I know?

Hatchard Homes Limited 2010-2019

This was the original generic name of the group and the core of the business. I had just left the Forces and the website was based on this. For the audited accounts trail my main bank account was with Natwest and the coaching and mentoring originally went through this account. I would take funds through one private account and send it to Hatchard Developments to develop directly. It was a bit archaic and clunky but it worked and my accountants in Bristol seemed to follow this ok for 12 years, or up until COVID-19. The administration process is now based on the ability to prove malfeasance with the unregulated lender pulling out of my projects as did a regulated pension company. The mission now was to rescind the administration process for all of the limited companies. This is a legal recovery process. This was not served notice or witnessed correctly and is now with the Legal Ombudsman.

Hatchard Developments Limited and Hatchard Construction Limited 2012 and 2015-2021

These two businesses did what they said on the tin. I tried to put one as the main developer and the other for maintenance. The refurbishment costs for the terraced houses in Wigan on average builds were approximately £16,000-£19,000. The semi-detached houses in Cornwall cost £75,000 to buy and about £55,000 to refurbish although this was set up differently on the bridging arrangement as I discussed before. The larger units back up in Wigan, 123 Bradshawgate had a spend of about £800,000, Platt Fold Street about £300,000 and 100 Lord Street about £1,874,000. All were through Hatchard Developments.

The maintenance side through Hatchard Construction was certainly not too onerous based on the quality of my builds both on the Wigan terraces and on the larger projects at 123 Bradshawgate, 100 Lord Street and Platt Fold Street. The properties in Cornwall, albeit with our extra additional work to improve units from the original builder, and the three main Wigan based buildings outlined above were overall very well built. These were so unlike Persimmon Homes who were being reported in the press at that time as having really poor leases and such poor quality of work. I think from memory the CEO of Persimmon tried to retire with a *£115 million* pay off despite the company's reputation at that time of poor build quality and poor leases. I was on £44 a day having achieved national industry awards and had developed great quality building all with full freeholds. It just did not seem right somehow.

The properties' main maintenance issues were blocked drains after completion which was largely due to sand and cement being washed away by tradespeople. Then it would normally just be the odd gutter and the shower or bath tiles failing. Also all the terraces had the Damp Proof Course which might fail. Builders would give a ten year guarantee and then disappear. Overall on a large £1 million to £2 million unit over seven years, the maintenance would rarely be more than £1,500 per annum and that included the ground floor shop in one building with the outside marine ply being repainted in waterproof paint every two years. Industry wise this was really low cost and was superb value.

Box Drop Limited, Toru Security Limited and Toru Recycling Limited 2020-2021

I have put these last companies together as they were set up during the pandemic as more entrepreneurial type enterprises. The two Toru companies were based on the Rich Dad Poor Dad founder's Robert Kiyosaki's middle name and were also based on what I saw in the coalfield town i.e. very poor policing and almost non-existent refuse collection and bad litter. Fly tipping was dreadful everywhere. I had a Dorset driving licence and could not use the local Wigan borough refuse centre as the officialdom stated I was fly tipping from Dorset! This was totally unworkable and we have now just had the International Global Warming Conference up in Glasgow with all the greenhouse emissions and the like whilst I got defamed from the council for fly tipping! I could not get teenagers to stow litter or the authorities to take my litter. This was the media versus the real world and there seems to me to be a disconnect somewhere. Maybe it was me having been on the frontline for too long and being too 'real world'?

On our larger buildings we tried to have recycle bins implemented by Wigan council but lazy tenants and drug addicts would hide items in the bins and pull everything out to retrieve their stash or whatever they had hidden. This made it unworkable. I did some small-scale dry cardboard and cooking oil recycling from Fat Sapper which worked well on the commercial property side. It was about volume versus transport costs.

Box Drop Limited i.e. the reverse name of Drop Box was set up as I saw many delivery van drivers in lockdown throwing parcels around, people not being in to receive the parcels or simply having the wrong address. I noted that 25% of their stock was not delivered so parcels were either taken back with the drivers or were left with shops or neighbours and overall there was a huge amount of theft. I also noticed that a lot of empty cardboard boxes were thrown out at the back of buildings and were not crushed down. Box Drop consisted of a green wheelie bin with a clasp lock on the top with a combination lock and two box metal sections at the back that could be bolted to the front of the property. It was easy then for any empty dry cardboard to be folded up and left for the delivery driver in the gap behind the attached wheelie bin and the house. His delivery chit would be barcoded with the right address, a photo of the right house and a four pin lock number. He would then take a photo of the parcel in the bin, then lock it shut and take any card away to put in a special section in his van. The result was that 100% of parcels were delivered to the right houses. There was no theft, no damage and the parcels were kept dry.

This book in many ways is very blunt and to the point. From my side there have been plenty of mistakes, errors, bad luck and ignorance and in many areas I could have changed and done better. I was certainly very educated in property investing, mindful of the classroom and able to adapt to a very harsh environment but I also believe I was certainly naive and immature after my farm background and was not street wise. University and a military career in many ways cosseted me from the real world although leaving service when the 2008/2009 recession set in did not help with my timing but then I have never known any other environment. As said before, the military can be very one dimensional, self-centred and extremely focused when on operations so you do not have the 'noise' of normal life getting in the way. I kept persisting but my reaction times to events in COVID-19 was very slow particularly once the banks began to restrict back in 2015 and on the smash and grab in 2020 and 2021. This could be seen in the crash selling of my properties from the action of Together Finance and Duff & Phelps and later Whitehall Pensions and JB Leitch which was spectacularly vicious in its speed and severity. I was always very slow to come back. People commented on my poor email traffic and communication which I put down to the cumulative exhaustion which built up as 90 to 110 hour weeks were the norm for over 24 months. Lawyers and clients seemed to have me in their sights as I was constantly being attacked and viciously brought down to earth. The jungle is the survival of the fittest. I probably gave too much and was certainly unable to negotiate on finance restrictions. I also had so much on as a one man band and I had to get staff costs down quickly and be able to manage unskilled locals who were apparently unable to do simple tasks. In hindsight I definitely needed more technical support, admin, book-keeping and legals from the start. I was very poor on my contracts and templates used, the ones which so many start ups use and any chinks in the armour soon became very apparent in COVID-19. My use of technical skills overall was weak however, I was always very lean. When losing everything it is interesting how one's definition of lean changes. Lawyers have commented on this and could not believe that I administered 11 businesses from a one bed apartment, a modest car, a computer and a phone on £44 a day.

So what? I have included all the gross turnovers of all the limited companies to be transparent. And additionally to give you an idea of the sheer scale of the onerous work to be able to gain any form of lending plus all the Assets and Liabilities for more security.

'All the adversity I've had in my life, all my troubles and obstacles, have strengthened me... you may not realise it when it happens, but a kick in the teeth may be the best thing in the world for you'.

Walt Disney

23

The Survivor

I hope the farm and the military sections and the main small and medium sized business and property sections have given a flavour and a potted history of the build up to the damage of the financial sector to individuals and SMEs. I am adding a few anecdotal items to help draw the book to a close and give you the opportunity to come to a conclusion in your own mind. And also to give you some ideas that could help you in your attitude to life, conflict and hardship.

As you saw before, the Hatchard group was running circa £50,000 per calendar month gross turnover. Twenty months into COVID-19 as I write, the per calendar month turnover figure is now down to £1,351 i.e. it is now just my military pension at £44 a day. Now include the £6 million of lost buildings and the TM01 Companies House action potentially lost on 11 limited companies valued at £1.5 million and the lost lease on the warehouse and associated potential equity of £600,000. This was £9 million to minus £3 million in 18 months. Well done Together Finance, Duff & Phelps and Whitehall Pensions along with Wigan Court and the HMRC system. £44 pounds a day to live on which I have coped with for many years but now I have absolutely no savings or buffer. How can I overcome this, how can I survive? How could you survive?

The day to day existence on site was a bit bleak to say the least. I had broken gearboxes in the back of the car, I was manning the Covid 19 Busters shop during the day and covering the take out, Fat Sapper, at night. I was drying clothes that I had hand washed in the back of the estate car in the sunshine. Often I had £2.00 to get through from Monday to the following Friday as the Fat Sapper Just Eat income was delayed a week from the last trading period and I would still have to do the payroll. Then I remembered eating cattle feed, oxo cubes and jelly cubes on the farm and that onion on my Commando escape and evasion course, and I recalled the Vietnam POWs stories. Just get on with it 'H'. I had several occasions when the administrator had closed all the accounts down and I could not access any funds and additionally my military pension went missing for seven weeks at one point. The pandemic has been hard for a lot of people; always expect the unexpected.

It was so hand to mouth and it was really a dreadful time. I thought about selling my 21st gold watch, my military sword and my medals to make the payroll. They were happily 'taken' off me as 'gifts' from people. From October to December 2021 cash flow was non-existent and I was scouring the supermarket car parks for coins (CCTV would have a man in a blue jacket doing this). On a rare trip back home my daughter gave me £40 of her pocket money to fuel the car to get me back on site, she winked and told me aged ten 'to stare forward and not glance back on the damage'.

I was having regular pinch points because of the Just Eat payment weekly cycle and the pension issues. Sometimes I had to go to the pharmacy to see if they would just sell me three days of individual pills from my prescription for my serious DVT condition. I subsequently found out that this is a discretionary service. One nice chap did this over several months then the pharmacy owner came in one day and refused. I only needed three pills for £2.00 to get me through to Friday. No was the answer, so I told the chap I would need to go to A&E. I was really annoyed now. I was now having to count out individual tablets due to the total lack of resources I had caused by selfish lenders pulling the finance. I was pretty desperate to be bluntly honest. On the following Friday the Just Eat income coincided with the pension which meant I could go back and get my full prescription. The main owner I don't think registered. He didn't blink an eye - he would have done well at the Hanoi Hilton in Vietnam as a guard or a banker or a fee chasing lawyer. Move on 'H'.

Finally, let's finish the chapter on the smash and grab. The banks, pension companies, the lawyers, the courts and the odd investor (most investors were amazing considering the situation), just smashed into me. This was absolutely not helped by the lack of limited company law protection due to the unregulated lending set up in our own names. The day to day piece was where my main focus was and I now had no resources. I had to do what I could on my own. There was no extra finance or resources so legals were now the odd pro-bono advice with local firms who were helpful in small doses. Thank you all. There are *good people* out there, you need to find them.

At the mid-level there was a clear situation where I had large visible buildings and people would try it on with a smash and grab scenario. As previously mentioned on my new build from five years ago, the party wall dispute, 'Jazz Hairdressers' took two of my companies to court and 'won' £36,000 for a small mark in an adjoining wall. Thankfully that company and the legals are now being investigated by the Legal Ombudsman. Greed, sheer greed. Those hairdressers are not good business people.

Likewise, at the large warehouse we had a supposed tenant in about March 2021 stating that his new van with all his tools had gone missing. He then magically got an 'eye witness' account to state that the van was around in September 2020 and he wanted his rent from September to March repaid as this 'theft' had damaged his business. He also wanted the van and the tools paid for. There was no crime number and there was no valid insurance. This was totally and utterly unbelievable. My conveyancing solicitor then advised just to come away from everything. She was the one who had to crash sell all the £6 million of properties and lease agreements, after months and years of me having no proper exit bank lending with expensive bridging being pulled and now all this company, individual and personal family damage. She suggested to let it all go and let the greedy sharks feed and that there was going to be potentially nothing left anyway after the court costs and legal action. She suggested among other things to whistleblow, do a media campaign, write a book and get it all back having asked the Legal Ombudsman and local MP and Parliamentary petition to investigate and also help others. This is a large theme of the book.

So what? We will let the courts, the Legal Ombudsman and the Financial Ombudsman be the judge of all this and hopefully it will help others who have been treated similarly or who are struggling with comparable problems.

So what? I do hope readers will now be incredulous as to what has quietly been happening to individuals in business and people paying for goods and services not received.

And one final point, the insurance cover that I took out over twelve years has been absolutely not fit for purpose. The fraudulent leases on the purchase on 123 Bradshawgate were not covered in the Professional Indemnity and the main home had storm damage in 2019 which was never covered, both insurances were paid for. Professional Indemnity never covered the builder's poor standards of construction in Cornwall but I had paid the insurance cover for this. The Professional Indemnity was not covered on the claim on the party wall on 2-4 Brown Street North as in the three months of the actual claim date, in a policy held for over 144 months, the policy was mysteriously missing. The Legal Ombudsman is investigating this fraudulent claim. The claim on the Professional Indemnity on the gross RICS undervaluation on 100 Lord Street was paid for but yet was not covered. Insurers may argue this, I will let you the reader and the public decide. How many insurance policies during COVID-19 have not been paid out on claims?

Just so that I get a sense of balance on my growing anger here, society, business and individuals seem to have been paying for nothing. It sounds again like the finance we tried to borrow and keep and for which I paid at 17-27% APR, which was some *270 times* the base rate of 0.1 % APR, was all for nothing.

Just remember, when soldiers defend and go to war for you all (which we all pay for and why taxes were ever raised in the first place), they go without any quibbling, with no extra fees and no stupid excuses. They just do, they carry out their duties and execute the military covenant insurance in full for Her Majesty The Queen (and possibly in the near future, His Majesty, the King), and for the politicians on behalf of our country. Many of these people at such high risk in combat do all this with salaries ranging from £25,000 to £65,000 per annum on the front line; pretty cheap insurance I think. Some people have queried my own military covenant and my integrity, which I hope has now been covered in the front part of the book. (Recorded).

'The one thing I regret was that my work required an enormous amount of my time, and a lot of travel'.

Neil Armstrong

24

Calling for Government Investigation

Fat Sapper, just as we conclude below, wants an investigation especially over the treatment of SMEs and individuals and small property owners by the banks, their lawyers and the courts processes. The very sad suicide cases of Mike Norcross and indeed increasing other financial led suicides are extremely sad indictments of how things could have been handled so differently by finance houses, courts and lawyers in 2020-2021.

The exceptional reporting by the BBC, the 'i' newspaper and the Times should now prove to the UK public to be the tip of the iceberg. The sheer damage certainly to commercial property as per the Essential Information EIG auction group which reported a 369% increase in distressed commercial sales and 71% of distressed residential sales in mid 2021. It has to say something to the authorities about what has really been happening to individuals who have been treated by these same authorities with such contempt. We will allow the reader discretion on their own thoughts on this as I conclude.

We do not want another generation to allow finance houses to get away with making even more profits from people's misery either for individuals, families or their hard earned businesses during the COVID-19 era. The BBC report on the RBS GRG case 'give them more rope to hang themselves' is hardly a good epitaph for an already renowned greedy industry.

Finally The Prime Minister, Chancellor, Business Secretary and all MPs of the House must instigate a full investigation to not allow this to happen with the next downturn of the economy. 2008/2009 was ignored, if we allow 2020/2021 to be ignored yet again, we will undoubtedly then fall into another major recession. That would surely show a complete failure of the Government system to protect the small man and woman and business owners struggling against the banks, courts and lawyers. Four million of them – they are all voters.

'A banker is a fellow who lends you his umbrella when the sun is shining but wants it back the minute it begins to rain'

Mark Twain

25

Closing Thoughts

My service to my country, I was really proud of my military career as all ex-military servicemen and women are hence the lengthy outline at the start so you can get a measure of me in my approach to business. I will outline again the total achievements of 18 years military service with commendation. Two years with the airlines then 12 years in business, a total GDV of £7,850,000, total gross rents of £522,000, 90,000 sq. ft. of property developed. Likewise up to COVID-19 I was very proud to serve the property and small business industry, 200 rental units (including self storage and parking units), 144 tenants kept going via COVID-19, 12,000 sets of PPE sold, 2,000 students coached and mentored, 2,700 cars disinfected, 20 units offered for NHS emergency accommodation during COVID-19, 30,900 hot meals cooked by the take out Fat Sapper, five UK landlord awards, two UK small developer awards, two International Development nominations; 123 Bradshawgate and 100 Lord Street, International Mentor award worldwide covering 25 countries, 51 investors up until COVID-19 serviced and 32 plus creditors, 144 units cleaned and maintained, 1,000 plus overseas bank accounts set up for overseas investors, two published business books, £6 million of forced GDV sales including the lease option, *£1,485,000* of business rates and council tax *paid back into Wigan borough* on 200 units refurbished on the empty units (including self storage and car parking) and 11 limited companies from medium operations to start ups. All of this has been fully recorded. In eighteen months with COVID-19 this Assets 'A' sheet of £9.047 million plus business went to minus £3.5 million because of the lender pulling out finance and wanting his umbrella back when it started to rain. In twelve years I did not take a single penny or wage from the business. This is how I believe we should build houses, homes, businesses, towns and nations. With a UK base rate of 0.1% APR and twelve years of business totally wasted this was now 'financial cannibalism' on an epic scale.

Subject to the Legal and Finance Ombudsmans' investigations and Durkan Trustee work potentially we are helping the Secretary of State for Business and Liverpool Official Receiver to recover all of the above assets and annul and rescind Hatchard against Together Finance, Duff & Phelps, Whitehall Pensions, Wigan Court and HMRC. I have to pay my investors back in full as well as my creditors and then add to that the £12,000 I have raised to military charities to date. If it takes me another 12 years on £44 a day then that is what I must do. Just a 'soldier' doing his job. The proceeds of this book will go to investors and creditors first then a proportion to military charities afterwards.

At the time of writing we are being told that COVID-19 has killed 150,000 plus people in the UK and 5.5 million worldwide. You and I are still here by definition. For myself the terminal cancer of finance, courts, lawyers and total individual greed is really only now appearing and it is a particularly virulent form of cancer, where maybe it mutates to a severe form. Like the incredible scientists who all around the world found a COVID-19 cure, I really hope this book starts a process to do the same and find a cure for our finance, legal and court cancer, to help businesses and individual citizens survive, and be able to come back from this financial mess to serve our communities, our families and our nation again. There are some amazing people mentioned in this book. There are great people out there and even those with legal advice who sought to damage me, I still think deep down they are good folk. Forgive and forget.

There are 200 towns and cities with no commercial or shop lending, RICS are crash selling pensions and the UK has a base rate of 0.1% APR. Let the government and the authorities ask the 345 UK finance houses, why? This investigation needs to be retrospective in its scope to allow the treatment of others to be looked into. If not these towns and communities are dead forever. It will be a dark day if a generation loses its flair for entrepreneurialism and business because of all this.

The Prime Minister, Chancellor, Governor of the Bank of England, UK Business Secretary, Metro Mayors and Constituent MPs have really got to sort this out with a definitive SME banking, finance and legal investigation of what has happened to citizens, veterans and small businesses leading up to and during COVID-19 with lenders, brokers, lawyers and court actions.

I don't want my children to suffer yet another generation where they say that's just what the banks do when economic hardship occurs. It is the banks themselves who through each cycle cause all the unnecessary damage. It is pure greed, simple as. There has to be another way just as science and the UK NHS and other countries did with the COVID-19 vaccine research and dispensing.

I would take everyone of you on my 'average' military missions all over again but never, never ever to have to go through what myself, my family, my friends, military and civilian investors have had to suffer in my business through COVID-19. I did not want to write this book - I just wanted my family back.

It has been absolutely frightening and humiliating.

That from an average man who went to war four times. The people I served under and the '56' whose lives my team saved and '34 and more' we lost were the exceptional ones. They, two and a half million veterans, four million business owners, my team and investors deserve better from me.

I have the honour to be your obedient servant.

'Fat Sapper'

JPH

26

Lessons Identified

Throughout the book I have listed the 'so what's?' I have tried to tie the farm and military into the business in the first 20% of the book then tie the other 80% business back into the farm and military experience to see if there was any correlation to help anyone struggling through COVID-19 and Brexit.

Lessons identified:

a. Why are PayDay loans advertised at 1,500% APR in the mainstream media?

b. Unregulated Lenders. Principal Private Residence (main home) security requirements make them exempt from investigation. Why?

c. On forbearance why are bridging lenders' rates at 170-270 times the Bank of England base rate which is currently at 0.1%? Immediate pull of loans under duress and lack of forbearance and rates then increased 45%-75% during COVID-19. Greed.

d. Financial Conduct Authority, Financial Ombudsman, Serious Fraud Office, Citizens Advice Bureau, Trading Standards, British Banking Resolution Service and Legal Ombudsman. Are they fit for purpose?

e. Courts and Legal Process with COVID-19 protocol remote practice where individual citizens on their own on calls and emails and 'in court'. Is this fair?

f. Legal Ombudsman taking 13 weeks to answer. Why? Not fit for purpose.

g. Government legislation in the landlord property world was set at six months eviction moratorium on residential tenants and nine months eviction moratorium on commercial tenants. Tenants simply blackmailed owners, landlords and landladies over access knowing full well this would damage lending. Why discriminate against business owners if lenders then pull the loans? This will now involve years of expensive litigation. Tenants and workers had far better treatment than owners. Be at least fair to everyone.

h. Why were charities in properties being displaced?

i. Smart metres in property in the UK is a total mess right now. Discuss.

j. 68,000 homeless in the UK in the 21st century. Why? A national disgrace.

k. Council departments' treatment of SMEs and individuals. All 343 local authorities' treatment of small business and grants applications are needing a thorough investigation. Not fit for purpose, especially blocking of funding. Why are businesses doing the job of the Valuation Office Agency? Many council departments are not working through COVID-19. Not good enough. The disconnect between Central and Local Government.

1. VAT has to be flat rated to zero for builders to enable brownfield sites and empty buildings to be brought back into use and house families and businesses cost effectively.

*'Nearly all men can stand adversity,
but if you want to test a man's character,
give him power'.*

Abraham Lincoln

Appendix 1

Live Hatchard References and Current Investigations and Helplines

This has the UK Government regulated authorities contacts and pending regulatory investigations ongoing with references in my own business group:

Financial Conduct Authority	Ref #206907587
Financial Ombudsman	Ref #10183176
Serious Fraud Office	Ref #XMV1
Citizens Advice Bureau	Ref CL 102442361
Trading Standards	Ref Telecon/ no email audit
British Banking Resolution Service	Ref BBRS 3330
Legal Ombudsman	Ref 092087 - pending 13 weeks returns
The Pensions Ombudsman	Ref CAS - 83795- T6J9

Legal Ombudsman investigations: Jackson and West, Duff & Phelps, Clarke Wilmott, Bennet Williams, Wigan and Yeovil and Bath Courts, Together Finance Limited, JB Leitch, Whitehall Pensions and HMRC, Battens, DAC Beachcroft and Durkan Trustees for Secretary of State for Business. Durkan and Liverpool OR have supported well.

Rating (Coronovirus) and Director Disqualification
(Dissolved Companies) Act 2021

Royal Institute of Chartered Surveyors

Telecoms/ audited x 3 times ignored

Soldiers Sailors Airmen's Charity
www.ssafa.org

Alabare Veterans Homeless Charity
www.alabare.co.uk

Combat Stress
www.combatstress.org

White Ensign
www.whitensign.co.uk

Royal British Legion
www.britishlegion.org

Help for Heroes
www.helpforheroes.org

Royal Navy and Royal Marine Charity
www.rnrmc.org

RAF Benevolent Fund charity
www.rafbf.org

Good Samaritans Suicide Watch
www.samaritans.org

'Remember that there is nothing stable in human affairs; therefore avoid undue elation in prosperity, or undue depression in adversity'.

Socrates

Appendix 2

Developing History 2009-2021: Solicitor, Tax Accounts, Records, GDV and Turnovers

2009-2010

> 18 Wigan Terraces purchase £40,000
> Together Finance sales £78,000
> Refurbishments £18,000-£20,000
> Rents £450 pcm

2010-2012

> St Eval 8 Semi-detached buy £75,000
> Rented then sold £155,000
> 1-3-5-7-9 Warwick 2-4-6 Hudson
> £650 rents profits £20,000 each

2009-2015

> Gosport and Portishead Bristol
> Sold 2015-2016
> Estuary Hse, Marlboro, Netley, Serle
> Rents £650 pcm, Portishead £20,000

2013-2015

> 123 Bradshawgate
> Together Finance forced sales £800,000
> £400,000 buy and £400,000 refurb
> GDV's RICS values £225,000, £295,000,
> £495,000, £855,000, £925,000
> £82,500 rents pre-COVID-19

2014-2015

> New build plot of land
> Together Force sales
> Nil plus refurb £126,500
> Sold £140,000.
> S106 Wigan Council claim £12,000 plus

2014-2016

> Platt Fold Street
> 4 x 5 year leases
> Hatchard Homes Limited Administration rescind app

May 2021

> Up to date rents
> OR Liverpool - Avonside case
> Pension GDV £1.1 million
> Lease GDV potential £1,675,000
> Rents £100,000/£140,000 full use

2016-2020

> 100 Lord Street
> Rents gross £172,500
> £400,000 and £1,474,000 build
> Together Finance forced sale 2020
> Reserve set £1,050,000
> Sold £1,270,000
> Correct RICS GDV £1,900,000

Limited Company Basic History TM01 Action Ongoing

BBSSL	BOOST	HDL	HCL	COVID 19 B
£125,264	£115,000	£21,784	£24,149	£10,988
PA FIGS £400,000	FY 2018	£1,874,	000* Lord S	

FAT S	CENT'N	HHL	BOOKS	3 LTD
£139,000	£18,316	£140,000	£4,995	***
BBL54K	G'S £40,000	TERR'S	£200,000 #2 BK	TS TR BD

'People who fail focus on what they have to go through; people who succeed focus on what it will feel like at the end'.

Tony Robbins

Appendix 3

Table of Books -
Used In All My Businesses

1. 100 Business Lessons Learned from Brexit and Covid
    – J.P Hatchard
2. The Best Real Estate Advice I Ever Received
    – Donald Trump
3. Rich Dad poor Dad – Robert Toru Kiyosaki
4. Who Moved My Cheese – Dr Spencer Johnson
5. How To Make Friends and Influence People – Dale Carnegie
6. ABC of Real Estate Investing - Ken Mcelroy
7. Art of The Deal – Donald Trump
8. 10X Rule - Grant Cardone
9. Goals! - Brian Tracy
10. 7 Pillars of Wisdom – T. E. Lawrence
11. Think and Grow Rich - Napoleon Hill
12. Personal Memoirs – General Ulysses Grant
13. Chickenhawk – Bob Mason
14. Soldier Five - Mike Coburn

Appendix 4

Influencers -
Used In All My Businesses

1. Landry's - Tilman Fertitta
2. Starwood – Barry Sternlicht
3. 10x – Grant Cardone
4. VaynerMedia – Gary Vaynerchuk
5. Mindset - Tony Robbins
6. Progressive - Mark Homer
7. USA Real Estate - Greg Dickerson
8. UK Business - James Sinclair
9. UK Investing Real Estate – Ranjan Bhattacharya
10. Clinical Psychologist - Jordan Peterson
11. Rich Dad - Robert Kiyosaki
12. Management - Ken McElroy
13. Philosophy - Jim Rohn
14. Success - Darren Hardy
15. General Finance - Graham Stephan
16. Valuetainment - Patrick Bet-David

Parliamentary Petition title #603370 and MP James Grundy case number JG 123395

'Hold a public enquiry into unfair business practises during the pandemic'.

Pending 100,000 signatures.

Glossary

AAC -   Army Air Corps
APR -   Annual Percentage Rate
CAM -   Common Area Maintenance
CCT -   Combat Camera Team
CIL -   Community Infrastructure Levy
             is a levy that local authorities can choose
             to charge on new developments in the area.
CMA -   Competition and Markets Authority
CSAR -   Combat Search and Rescue
CTC -   Commando Training Centre
FOD -   Foreign Object Damage
FRI -   Full Repairing and Insuring
GDV -   Gross Development Value
HMCG -   Her Majesty's Consul General
HMO's -   House of Multiple Occupation
IED -   Improvised Explosive Device
IRT -   Immediate Response Team,
             Helicopter Rescue Aircraft aka US 'Dust Off'
LGW -   London Gatwick
LTV -   Loan to Value
MOE -   Monthly Operating Expenses
MPAN -   Meter Point Administration Number
NAS -   Naval Air Squadron
PCM -   Per Calendar Month
POW -   Prisoners of War
RAF -   Royal Air Force
RM -   Royal Marine
RN -   Royal Navy
RNAS -   Royal Naval Air Station
ROI -   Return on Investment
ROTI -   Return on Time Invested
RFA -   Royal Fleet Auxiliary
RMAS -   The Royal Military Academy Sandhurst
RNAS -   Royal Naval Air Station
RSME -   Royal School Military Engineering
Sappers - Royal Engineers i.e. British Army Engineers

SAS -   Special Air Service
SBRR -   Small Business Rates Relief
SBS -   Special Boat Service
SERE -   Survival, Evasion, Resistance and Extraction
SFO -   Senior First Officer
SHOL's - Ships Helicopter Operation Limits
SME -   Small and Medium-Sized Enterprises
SNCO -   Senior Non-Commissioned Officer
SOE -   Special Operations Executive
SOOTAX -Senior Officer Transfer
TOW -   Tube launched, optically tracked,
                 wire guided missile on a Lynx Aircraft
WMD -   Weapons of Mass Destruction
UAV -   Unmanned Aerial Vehicle